v v v

& Rainbow

v v v

Contents

[Rebecca Friend]

If Only

Heat waves in winter
tilt
southern spheres
off-kilter and
wilt the forest fringe,

tiny stalactites of ice
that trickle
an arrhythmic tap
matching
lopsided lurches of
my porch swing

and I'm sitting
stoned and sleeveless at
midnight

counting yellow kernels
burning overhead
as starlight
pops.

Night air crawls,
warm for December
and I hear conifers
whistle,

a breathy chorus of
treetop trios

harmonizing with
the hum of crickets,

they croon of
spring's early
debut,
roses in June
moonlight tokes,
mint-lemonade scented
kisses.

If only.

I know about the
come and go
of snow,
can tell that swelling
welcome chorus
that more squalls
hide

sheltered by these
cockeyed breezes,

how frozen whiteness
invades wheat fields
heartbeats

and bedsheets,

that life is a
dealer
with muscular arms,
a cold shoulder and
wandering eyes
snatched
from blue skies.

Mother, grandmother, social worker and storyteller from
North Carolina. I found my voice in poetry.
Allpoetry.com/Becki_Friend

[Paul Goetzinger]

The Old Mining Town

On a radiant day, autumn quilts sprawling wetlands with pastels of red and orange hues.
Awakening shrubs and grasses in peaceful repose, sprinkled in drifts of tiny daisies.

Hidden within deep shadowed hideaways, a small town rises from a restless slumber.
Flaunting aged buildings, covered with vertical jumbles of trees, evergreen and deciduous, towering upwards within timbered castle walls.
Blocking views of the outside world, like the top of a covered wagon.

On the banks of a desolate creek, young ducks rest on warm straw, soft downy feathers tucked close, tinted the color of plum, congregating in sunshine, watching for storms gathering in the west, living in a tiny settlement that is civilization.
Nearby, skittish mountain hummingbirds
Nurture solitary wild apple orchards
Clinging to hills above
Along deep fjords of rock and granite.

In obscure hallows, vivid echoes of a miners pick, and the roaring explosion of a dynamite blast, signaled the feverish search for earth riches, following the footsteps of faceless

adventurers seeking fortunes in dark passages, illuminated by candlelight.
Spawning a roaring boomtown.

Where hopeful dreams bore aspirations of striking it rich, where cabins were built, bridges were erected, and a small general store sold merchandise to eager prospectors.
Many gave up, left for the lowlands, took up raising livestock, planting crops, seeking more productive riches of the earth.

Others stayed, leaving honeycombed tunnels and holes in rugged mountains and valleys, harboring secrets of lost wealth and lifetimes of labor and frustration, vainly hoping for glory holes yielding great sums.
In winter, heavy blizzards created virile snow-slides pouring down canyons, demolishing buildings, burying inhabitants alive.

The town is gone
Now inhabited by lonesome highways, tumbleweeds, canyons, coyotes and free range cattle.
Nothing but broken boardwalks and decaying buildings, where feverish mining activity flourished on the edge of the frontier.
Where nature has painted high alpine meadows, bursting with lupine and Indian paintbrush
And a turquoise blue glacier, dancing happily in the tinged sunlight.

Where time yields to a timberline sky-world of grasslands and snowfields, smooth as a fresh ironed bedsheet in the morning, snagging wandering clouds, white capped and furious.
Walking miles through stately Douglas firs, pink and orange colored granite walls loom, their rocky slopes distant on the horizon, exposing rocks and flowers of wild berry plants burnished in fall colors.

Through the foothills of autumn's stage, a pair of fawns stand vigilant, frozen like lawn ornaments, and a ribbon waterfall, rising behind an indigo pool, protects tempestuous shores, as wind whips along a lake, turning its glassy surface into turbulent waves, while finely dressed mountain goats defy gravity on sheer, rock strewn walls.

As sunset closes its nocturnal hand, fluted ridges glow with pink shine and reach upwards to Himalayan heights.
Giving back to night its deep shadowed hideaway

Paul Goetzinger is an educator and writer from Des Moines, Washington. He uses poetry to inspire and mentor his students. Allpoetry.com/Paul_Goetzinger

[Alwyn Barddylbach]

But for the Mirror of Eternal Grace

If we'd embrace the Gandhi among us
this savage world would be a better place.
They said if the universe is conscious
a star can shift in space, so I wondered if

the cosmos could be kind enough despite
the human race. Can a river find its
maker, an ocean mind its brood? Can cloud
blind a mountain, its godly goodness chase?

I may sit and trace my thoughts that I might
remember them without drowning in my
own reflection. I may displace the air
above to face the storm they throw at me, but

can I bind the hand that takes my only
breath away? Entwined about my heart like
some grand old staircase designed for the crowd
but for this mirror of mortal stone I yield,

I yield its grace.

Earth speaks if we have ears to listen. Tribute to Mahatma
Gandi (1869 - 1948). Wish or covenant, symbol of humanity
and grace, AB Blue Mountains Australia.
Allpoetry.com/Barddylbach

[Michael Mogel]

Summer Harbor Fall Shore

Morning sea invades the pier
with a growl it gulps the wooden legs that sway high tide.
The migratory fish feed
among the weeds; and boys with worms and lines play tag
up on
the pier. The flapping chilly bass with swelling
gills are picked up by the tail - dropped
in canvas sacks to die. The boys withdraw
when fish dart away. Then low noon tide
leaves slime on the pier where salted wooden
planks sun dry until high tide.
Sun browned grass growing in the sand
bends death like
as if praying for a merciful intermission.
The fall invasion wastes no time.
Rocks jounce on blowzy glass; above the sea
smashed shells the seagulls hunt
trapped small fish and junk from picnics
left last June. A dory moored against
the waves slams a quay whose old gray boards
twist and creak; the bracing poles stand firm.
Boat shaped clouds drift by
unseen by
boys and girls parked at the pier.
Salted wind blows down
and down the wet weed shore and smooths the glass

that's made from sand, sandblasts the junk, and turns
the shells to dust.

Michael Mogel, born in Boston Massachusetts, writing helps
me express my souls itching into concrete image - it also
helps me cope with Parkinsons. I also play guitar and am a
motorcycle rider. Allpoetry.com/Writesummer66

[Jack Mullen]

Young Sailor Sings

Pour forth the best you've got, Trade Wind,
or send your worst.
Wide stanced I roll with heaving deck,
fist gripped on mains'l halyard,
shake with laughter the other in your teeth.

Green water surges 'round me
each time we plunge our bow
through swelling surf.
I face cold salt spray's stinging bite
to know I'm full alive!

Proud ship and I, one upon the mighty sea,
have harnessed you, sail and rudder, with ease

Together we tamed Mediterranean ways,
mastered cold mistral's north'ly might
flailing French winter in our face,
tacked 'gainst levanter 's unyielding easterly gale,
sank Gibraltar in our wake.

Challenged North Atlantic's fabled winter winds,
Sailed round The Horn both ways and braved
Magellan's Strait to Pacific shores and back,

Melted salt free chunks from floating ice berg mountain.

Now, famed trades, with you we gloat blue watered ways
cargo filled for home,
full proof we've heard and loved
your sweet voice ringing through our lines and stays.

––––––––––––––––––––

Jack Mullen lives retired in College Station, Texas with his
wife Margie of 60 years. He enjoys doting on grandchildren
and great-grandchildren, pondering nature and family life.
Allpoetry.com/Jack_Mullen

[Rebecca Friend]

A few words about the past century

The hands of my
grandparents
fostered children
outside
their farmhouse,

golden soldiers
straightened by
shafts of sun and
raised
in the mountain
slopes of
Appalachian irrigation.

Rows of buckwheat,
barley and
grinning yellow maize
waved and played
hide and seek
with pink cheeked
half-siblings,

offspring different but
the same,
tall and rooted in
soil muddied

by rain and family
blood.

My grandparents' eyes
saw only the
sunrise,
day to day visionaries
they carried mornings
in milk buckets,

counted chicken eggs
and pennies for
winter's cease-fire,

husked a hundred
harvested ears,

whispered lullabies at dusk,

tucked babies into
bunkers of quiet and
quilted nights.

The land of my
grandparents
turned about-face,
sprouted tract
housing and
boxwood boundaries,

real armies and
neighborhoods without trees,

asphalt sealing the
cornfield they walked
seeing
only green,
each other and the
sunset colors
signaling
another tomorrow.

Mother, grandmother, social worker and storyteller from
North Carolina. I found my voice in poetry.
Allpoetry.com/Becki_Friend

[John Lars Zwerenz]

Nostalgia

When the purple drapes of the nascent night
Cover the veils of the mountainous greenery,
I wander amid the fountains and the statuary,
Lost in reflective pools of light.

And when the moon ascends to the sobbing sky,
Alone in the starry firmament of black,
I recall the ringlets upon your smooth, white back,
When the spring evenings blessed us, you and I.

How profound was our felicity,
How deep was our joy,
When we danced in the meadow as girl and boy,
With an ardor that shone like diamonds on the sea.

Now the drab days slowly pass,
As I walk upon the wan, old grass,
Beneath the cradle of the weeping trees;
In the darnel, wavering, high, then low,
Through the wilting, tremulous reeds I go,
Haunted by your name, which scents the wild breeze.

John Lars Zwerenz is an American poet. He is widely
considered one of the most important literary figures of the
present era. He is the author of nine volumes of verse.
Allpoetry.com/John_L._Zwerenz

[Jack Mullen]

I Had Forgotten The Many Species Of Snow

First a flurry,
Specks, dots, powder;
Then real flakes surfing
Shorebound foam
on crashing waves of Arctic wind
whirling, swirling, diving,
a frenzy of random excitement.

Now, lazy particles
exploded featherbedding,
soar, and dip, and ride
A galaxy of miniature magic carpets,
released aloft in space,
heedlessly careening downward in lazy arcs
to cling to wire and branch
at last to rest and deaden sound
grown into clumsy glove and quilted vest
numbing visual memory into shapeless clumps.
I had forgotten the many species of snow.

Tomorrow,
stinging grains,
slanting freezing rain to sleet then snow.
Black iced roads and ways endangered, wind polished,
cleared and sanded, plowed and salted;
roadside dunes of frozen waste

layered in generations by steady shifts of giant trucks
driving relentless wedges of steel
into windblown drift and new fallen flakes.

While we sleep again,
fresh drifts begin the land anew
for exploration.

Night,
locked in silent arctic cold,
prepares unsullied lands for warriors,
kings and queens whose squeaky boot steps will trudge,
break fresh trails,
open new lands for discovery, conquest and dominion.

At dawn,
a moment for thought and memory,
and patience,
with knights and ladies,
who would refuse their armor
and rush to fields of conflict unfed,
before,
unabashed,
the sun with playful gesture,
prepares the place for forts and wars
and angel wings,
and fox and geese
and coal chunked eyes, and battered hat
and sleds and skis and
runny noses –

Years of lost and forgotten youth,
melted away with old snows and
snowmen glaring through lumps of coal
and trails of tag
and angel wings
and fox and geese
faded years, golden years,
reach past gas glowing street lights,
haloed in fresh falling flakes.

Freshness, whiteness, innocence
so quickly lost to soot and melt
first grizzled thaw pocked lumps
then mush and mud
and halting step and
"memory grown dim faded tone and tint"

New winter now
soul-less, aware-less,
rides in with splendor,
flurries and flakes!

sublimates,
crystallizes,
whitens,
cleans,

and refills the lungs
with confidence in self!

I had forgotten the many species of snow.

Jack is from College Station, Texas where he is retired with Margie, his wife of 60 years, Retired from the Army and public school teaching, he spends his time with poetry and extended family. Allpoetry.com/Jack_Mullen

[Arlice W. Davenport]

Cluny

French revolutionaries guillotined God at Cluny,
but He exacted His tithe all the same: one-tenth of their bad
ideas tossed back at them. The tyranny of terror, cheap
dream of heaven, in ruins.

A vast emptiness swamps the nave; stumps of pillars stained
black and gray and black again by age and rain and blood.
Only one tower stands intact. I scan the burnished hills
behind it; they do not look back.

"The birth throes of liberty," cried Thomas Jefferson.
"Rejoice!"
Despots toppled; authority crippled   for a future that never
comes.
Terror and waste; waste and terror. The desolation of faith.

On the tiny town square, a bistro beams. Syncopated lights
surge behind the bar, sending out distress signals of the
mind:
the throb of synapses firing wildly in the wind. *Material
infinity.*

Old men saunter in to down a beer,   and harness their dogs
under tables.
Parents and students sip pricey shots of espresso.
Emancipated energy.

Above the din, they cannot hear   the Earth's foundation crack.

Freedom leaves a sacred void in its wake,   watered by the blood of worldly martyrs. On the menu: *égalité, fraternité, fissure and ruin.*
Thunder in the hills. Words crash around us like cannonballs.

Liberté lingers outside in the municipal lot. A van propped up on wooden blocks for the night. No hassles, man. *Free parking.*
Let's hoist another beer to Robespierre. His dog strains at its leash.

Arliced is from Wichita, Kansas. Poetry lets me combine the power of image and idea in a single creation. I often include references to my travels in my poems. Both can help transport you beyond yourself. Allpoetry.com/arliced

[Rebecca Friend]

A special delivery

He wore that
redneck suntan of
an outdoors man,

two-toned arms
of burnished bronze
with white biceps,

face checkered by
freckles and red mud
acquired
after hours of

tucking seeds into flowerbeds

and carrying a
leather sack
stuffed
with love letters,
phone bills and
yellow flyers

house to house

when mail still
traveled on feet and

reached
hand to hand

in rain or snow or sleet.

I was his daughter,
his tomboy in
pigtails and ruffles
but father was my
frontier guide,

a pony ride in air
on shoulders
high as the sky,

a jumpstart
for an old Dodge Dart

and teacher of
tricks,
like the art of
tossing
horse shoes.

His hands turned
hardwood trees
into kindling,

could curl
an apple peel

into a perfect
spiral,

brought the world
to the
neighborhood
saving
the best parts for me.

Mother, grandmother, social worker and storyteller from
North Carolina. I found my voice in poetry.
Allpoetry.com/Becki_Friend

[Susmitha Muraleedharan]

Wisteria

Her slender shoulder laden
with the heft of newborn-vine
climbing cluster on flailing fence
lilac tresses in lavender raceme
the heave of replete honey
a boon for espying butterfly
hovering nearby ivory
lithe amaryllis petal-flurry

Under amethyst sky's rail
moonlit whets her apparel
violet garb to prattling purple
when slow breeze fiddle
unwinding her cavil
by pouring claret wine
to cobalt tumbler reed
over lips glossing ruby-red
in a candlelit eventide

_____

Sue is an engineer and lives in NC and her thoughts are
expressed by flowing words, can they be called poems, she
always wonder... Allpoetry.com/SubtleMist

[Laurie Grommett and Penelope Allen]
Fashion Falderal

We make our marks with exquisite fashion sense
right here, refined reaches down to the hem-line.
Distinctive dressing means signature style,
striking labels license a thunderbolt.
Haute couture guarantees an impeccable fit,
only mavens frequent our exclusive house.

Trendsetting speaks tailor made, designed in-house;
celeb collections are seamed with sultry sense.
Red-carpet rags with prices that don't fit
tags, clothe name-dropping stars walking the line.
Oscar chose Chanel gown beaded by the bolt
and one custom pearl encrusted strapless style.

We're the clothes-horses that canter with style.
On coltish legs, we raced out of the house.
High-heeled on catwalks, a jungle bolt
of feline fabric reveals our stalking sense.
Skirting fringes, we pirouette line by line,
while impresarios throw a pitched fit.

Paparazzi of live mannequins, formed and fit,
we focus on dollar figures and sell style.
Those poser portfolios would flatline
into frump without us rocking the house.
Shutterbugs, our lenses possess light sense,

fastening cutting-edge with flattering bolt.

Spring flings around the globe, fashionistas bolt
from pillar to post perusing each outfit.
Barely basted alterations leave a sense
of risky business. Autumn turns the style.
Each persnickety production crowds a house,
automatons file down the ensemble line.

Not so sweet "Seventeen" showcases our teen line
staging polls. Who wore a necklace made from a bolt?
Pubescent boys hide our spreads in their house.
Camel toes in Vogue would appear so unfit.
What's chic on frill street gives Cosmo and Elle their style.
Our glossy issues are ad-riddled nonsense.

Gurus of riches are rags line up fads to bolster house.
Knock-offs cost mere cents on the dollar-store bolt.
Spotlighted frippery fittings finance style.

Sestina collaboration. Pen Allen is a published poet from
Canada. She enjoys writing sestinas with Laurie and loves
rhyme. Laurie Grommett is a teacher from California who
pens varied poetry. Collaborations boost her art.
Allpoetry.com/L.G. Allpoetry.com/PenAllen

[Marta Green]

The Accipitral Fighter Pilot

White slicked back hair
large beak like nose
baggy black flight suit
flaps in the wind.

A fighter pilot gets in his jet
checking his wing flaps are set
getting up to speed to fly
before taking off into the skies.

Flame fired engines
gaining altitude until
smoking exhaust trail leaves
only a dot in the sky.

Straight nose dive down
like a Raptor after its prey
leveling off for a flight
to the island of Oahu.

Many miles out of the states
the fighter pilot prepares to land
on the USS Nimitz Aircraft Carrier
for a Pearl Harbor memorial day.

Getting in a landing pattern

wheels like talons come in sharp
gripping the tarmac
skidding to a stop.

—————————————

I have been married to my best friend for 10 years now who
makes me laugh to no end. My passions are family, animals,
especially writing, reading and art!
Allpoetry.com/Marta_Green

[Cheryl E. Martin]

Look to the Skies

A rotating cloud of gas and dust revolve
around the sun. The sun is sovereign
holding all its subjects in line.
Diminutive rocky planets and large
gassy spheres circling their ruler.

The earth rotates as it's
told. Winter turns to spring; which
turns to summer, and then to autumn.

Winter crystallizes a swaddle
of white to blanket the precious land
for impending growth.

Spring rains fall hard, or softly sprays
lands for saplings yet to swell,
and strengthens new vegetation
for the coming summer.

Summer brings pregnant lands bearing
fruit for humankind. Plucking purple berries,
orange fruits, and green lettuces fresh
from earth's land –
sweet and bitter on the tongue.
Creating jams for winter,
when the seasons circle around again.

Autumnal time offers leaves of red,
yellow, orange, and green. Decaying and giving
back to earth new soil for planting, as
spring will circle around once more.
Time to pluck apples from trees and
make juices, sauces, and pies to last through
hoary winter with its swaddle of white.

Round and round we spin on this ball
called earth. This planet held in space
by its leader – the sun. Round and round
the seasons spin on this sphere held in
space by its leader – the sun.

Each star, planet, moon –
aligned in perfect order.

_____

Cheryl E. Martin is from NJ. She's been married nearly forty years and practices yoga, hiking, biking, and walking.They are activities that clear her mind, and help her become a better writer. Allpoetry.com/Cheryl_E._Martin

[Alwyn Barddylbach]

Painting Clouds for Jack's Sake

Jack be nimble Jack be quick,
powder off a candlestick,
swifter than the driven snow
breathless angels watch him go.

Eira crystal star opaque
lighter than a candleflake,
softer than a feather make
painting clouds for Jack's sake.

Jack be nimble Jack be sad
needle footed lightly clad,
to the fells Jack did scamper
with elvish gad and damper.

Eira to the skies she flies
to look for Jack before he dies,
crystal stars and candleflake
painting clouds for Jack's sake.

Jack be nimble Jack be dead
counting silver on his head
in a meadow lightly spread
crusty as a loaf of bread.

Eira whiter than a swan

down to earth her feathers gone,
ev'ry hill and quarry cover
that Jack had frozen over.

Jack be nimble Jack be quick
powder off a candlestick,
crystal stars and candleflake
painting clouds for Jack's sake.

Flying over Moscow while London and Seoul were in the
grip of winter snow. Eira: Welsh name meaning snow.
Anglo-Welsh nursery rhyme touch the rainbow, AB 2011,
Blue Mountains Australia. Allpoetry.com/Barddylbach

[Stephen Hollins]

Raffled at Piha

I won the school raffle
Yahoo! I won a longboard
the luckiest kid in school
It fell off the back of a truck
had a crack in it, so what!
only cost me a 50 cent ticket

green and yellow with a red stripe
two fins dead flat no wax
Dad put it on top of the ranch wagon
driving west to Piha, the birthplace of
New Zealand surfing, singing the forest ranges

giant Lion Rock the coastal magician
sixteen million-year-old volcanic statue
greats us as we carve down a gravel hillside
charcoal sand burns feet in the hot sun
dries to a crunchy biscuit crust

surf sounds mirror a war going on
pounding cannons, rifle blasts, explosions
turquoise, white splashing glistening sea
heat vibrating off the beach
chips, milkshakes, colored umbrellas

running to the water with my brother

arms wrap board battling chill breeze
two boys not yet teenagers
skipping into the lion's jaw
sweet adventure dripping from lips

pounding waves roar ahead
deadly rips dark underground wings await
but what of this to our young heartbeats
dressed in long jeans and brave naked chest
while the surfers wear shiny black wetsuits

"Let me show you how to do it," I said
what was I thinking, I had never surfed
could hardly swim, dog paddle at best
but I had my longboard my mighty stallion
my 50 cent savior, 'Yahoo Pass the Breakers'

rehearsed in the back of the classroom
looking out the window waiting for the bell
Smash! the first wave pushed me clear off
no ankle straps no wax on board, 'Hold on Tight'
hero status dropped a few notches, quickly

30 minutes later I watched the board spin high
into the air, for the last time, my body tired
knuckles blue with cold, I had learned to swim
at least dog paddle but now washed and drained

the rip had me in her jaws waltzing me
to the jagged rocks for a jolly good pounding

something said
'let that stubborn sense of independence go,
call for help you dick head'
calling for 'Help!' I hear another yelling
a surfer smashed, bleeding, tangled in rocks

I'm next for the black magma shark teeth
lifeguard's voice screams 'Get on my board'
paddle, use your arms, swim if you want to live'
now my children have grown

bathing in the Piha sunset
orange, pink, red, purple
chill nights wrapped in the dark bush
diamond milky way, you can almost touch it
Piha lifeguards, guardians of the Iron Sands

Have fallen in love with writing poetry. Lives on Waiheke
Island New Zealand. Doting Dad, Actor, Theatre
Director/Teacher, Clown, Mime, Playback Theatre, Dancer,
Living Theatre Director, Builder.
Allpoetry.com/Stephen_Hollins

[Ryder Pittz]

Darkness on the Edge of Town

it's existed since
father time tipped the hourglass-
setting in motion the
golden sands-
hanging, fluttering like a veil,
prison walls closing in
upon the darkness on the edge of town.

The township expands
in all directions, stopping
at the Bastillian border.
I have walked all dead-end streets,
unable to press further on,
unable to pull himself away.

As a young boy,
there existed a hill
on 3rd and Maple.
standing atop the mound,
the vista beyond his wall
seemed attainable,
if only I could climb higher.

So, I planted a tree,
acquiring the seed from
the old man across the way.

My palms outstretched, the seed fell-
the man's hands brushed against mine,
like sandpaper,
with bandages taped over varicose veins.
He smelled near death:
greasy and of argyle sweaters.

the man's eyes followed me
as I rushed off the rotting porch,
though the eyes were kind,
they brimmed with loneliness
and half-crazed dementia.
He watched me run,
muttering as he turned back inside,
"cut it loose or let it drag
you down."

Atop the hill, the seed was sowed.
when I was sure of no listeners,
I whispered to the tree
stories of what we would see
together,
of what was beyond the veil.

The tree grew gnarled and bent,
decrepit houses and neighborhoods
demolished and replaced
with high rent condos and
fruit-based craft breweries.
the height of new buildings quickly

overtook.
Delighted, I scrambled up
circular staircases and
well-placed scaffolding.

Perched above the sky,
my illusion of what was beyond
shattered.
The veil extended into the clouds,
inducing the rain.
Wipers flash to and fro below,
cars stuck in traffic,
slowly disappearing into the shroud
that encloses my solitary confinement.

I slog home,
shoulders slumped with the
weight of the world.

Ryder was born and raised in Golden, Colorado, in the
shadow of the Rockies. He is studying Poetry at the
Metropolitan University of Denver.
Allpoetry.com/RyderPittz

[Marilyn Griffin]

Portrait 1966

Her black braided bun
like a balancing plate on her big beautiful head,
a glorious Cleopatra
Silk kimonos draped her white skin
a floral caftan of intricate delicacy
the glamping queen of first degree.
We'd stretch tents out on pegs
rough, wood stools and aluminum picnic tables
graced with frilly tablecloths
Stuffed cornish game hens
rice strewing out on gold plates
Sparkling bubbly lovely would spill over
our lips as we lisped and laughed
Her husband, made of aftershave and grass
tanned, with golf clothes never wrinkled
A mannequin among men
But She
She filled every room--she filled every
canyonlake and mountainvalley
We were babies and
I remember her.

Gardener, lover of books, ducks, chickens and puppies. I'm also a children's librarian and book seller! Love Jesus and my family, infinitely blessed!
Allpoetry.com/Greenautumn88

[Rebecca Friend]

Now she organizes the stars

She left a lacquered
jewelry case,
black satin lined,

a treasured space for
two pearl earrings and
her gold wedding
band,

a cardboard box of
photographs,
black and white
years
stacked in tens

hidden beneath
snapshots
sharpened by daylight's
exposure and
dawning colors.

Scenes of forest
green,
aquamarine seas and
blushing-pink
cheeks

but faces are creased,

aged by a thousand
viewings,
the touch of fingers
and deepening
wrinkles,

like her notecard
library of rotating
recipes,
gravy smeared,
dog-eared and
alphabetized,

the sheath dresses and
double-breasted
blazers,
steam-pressed and
threading
her cedar closet,

orderly and by category,

spring florals and
gingham on
quilted hangers
segregated from
winter wools,

memories of mother,
dust and cinnamon and
mothball scented

and all in their places.

_____

Mother, grandmother, social worker and storyteller from
North Carolina. I found my voice in poetry.
Allpoetry.com/Becki_Friend

[Aaron Ehrhart]

It Never Stays Organized

Into the Tupperware containers
the sugar, flour and olive oil goes
spice jars go in the revolving rack
silverware is thrown in the drawer

dish soap to the left of the sink
paper towels on a spindle
clean shirts hang within the closet
jeans are folded in the dresser
and dirty clothes litter my bedroom

while the bird screams in her cage
throwing seed all over the clean floor
sheets wrap my queen size bed
where I rest my now throbbing head

I go by the name Poetic Creations on AllPoetry.com and my
passion is writing, writing for me is a way of communicating
that which I fail to do with common speech.
Allpoetry.com/Poetic_Creations

[David I Mayerhoff]

What Was That Thing?

Sly as the devil
on stealth
eyeing the fruits
of plunder

Slithering like the
snake of fours
the fox
befriends no one
as it walks alone
through brush and thicket

Behemoths brush its sides
dwarfs skate past it
through the aisles
of forest

All outflank
or outmatch
this furry scavenger

The fox carries the driver's license
of the coyote
with creatures moving along
thinking the pack
close by

Stealing the eggs
from under the legs
of hens
neighborhood alert
with no idea
how it manages
in and out

To the small bird
it is the hyaena
without humor
to the driver
on high mountain road
it is the fur coat
running from traffic

Close to the ground
but never far
from trouble

———————————

David I Mayerhoff is an emerging writer while being a
practicing psychiatrist for the last 35 years. He is a Clinical
Professor of Psychiatry and a published author.
Allpoetry.com/David_Mayerhoff

[Paramita Roy]

The Routine

My busy father commences the 7th hour
of his thursdays
Punching a lotus bud into blooming,
Making aggressive eights
with the shaved sandalwood stub
on the cold, wet stone pata.

He then rummages through the polythene bag
of flowers
looking for a 5 or 7 leaf arrangement
of a mango whatchamacallit
(twig? branch?- translations are difficult)
and dots them with a red vermillion smear.
He scoops up a lot of gulal on his index finger-
dots the foliage, the pewter mug, the banana,
the A4 framed gods and goddesses- till
his finger runs dry, leaving nothing
but a red residue embedded in his
nail line.

Next he picks up a bunch of fine grass and
looks for the elusive three blade durba
(five of those)
from his lap full of heather.

He counts five unshelled rice grains and ALL

this he offers to Laxmi, the goddess of wealth and plenty-
before he can scarf down his breakfast and leave for his small
retail business- selling plain and sensible shoes.

The ritual over, he wears his shirt, combs his hair (bald patch and all)
then tells my mom- "Aschi" (leaving for now)

My mother waits at the balcony to see him leave.
He rarely looks up, bowed down by the weight of his toil.
like a beast of burden.
She waves anyway, chanting a little prayer for his well-being.

My father is an atheist, who believes in my mother.

―――――――――

is a slow growing poet. Poetry is all she's got. The only thing she is good at. She's also from Kolkata, India.
Allpoetry.com/Paramita_Roy

[Vicki Copp-Rutrenbeck]
vistadome

Denver to Chicago
twenty hours on train
landscape is flat, flat, flat,
360 degrees of flat

360 degrees of sky in vistadome
thirty minutes of lasting sunset
crane neck around to west
wispy lemon, gold, blistering carrot

above layers of vermillion
fiery cerise vibrant magenta
ahead to east bands of
turquoise royal blue deep purple

from horizon to horizon
drowning in color
spotlights of iridescent clouds
shadow the ground

1964 trip to family home
of my new husband

carried on a rainbow

Found AP on my birthday . . . a present to myself . . . this is
my niche . . . I am ever so happy . . . memories make the
best poems . . . but I wake up editing my dreams.
Allpoetry.com/Imagery1

[Ratul Banerjee]
Beautiful dream-catcher

Large window with beautiful glimpses of the world beyond
Where the bucolic landscape …..blue-green mountains roll
into
Lemon yellow meadows, tall willow, birch trees, shaded
outlines
Along the winding lanes cutting through the fields as dry
leaves
Remain fallen and at stray along the ground, end of August
And the air is very cool, resplendent, days are sun-drenched,
frilly
Happy days are here again! and alongside the tapestries
hanging from the window is the dream-catcher hoop
The ethnic, a family heirloom originating from the American
Ojibwa Chippewa Lakota tribe
Splendor as colored feathers hang from the hoop with
legends' connectivity, the spider's web manifestation
My beautiful dream-catcher, the hoop lightly sways in the
breeze
Should wondrous dreams come yet again, as this ethnic
"spider"
As it filters all dreams, come what may, good or bad,
through its gleaming white cobwebs
As good dreams pass through and bad dreams, it destroys
trapping and burning it down by the sunlight enigma
Beautiful ethnic dream-catcher, the faith I restore on you
Every nightfall and every morning advent, I have no worries

As I sleep peacefully and my dreams, of course, I am well guarded
By this iconic talisman, the ethnicity the dream-catcher

Ratul is from Kolkata India. She has taken up writing as a favorite pastime and is also fond of painting , likes to listen music . To her poetry is the right interface of communication with the world. Allpoetry.com/Ratul_Banerjee

[Lisa F. Raines]

Breathe

We cooperate
to collaborate,

so as not to abrogate
our responsibilities

to those we need,
and heed, and feed;

to live a life,
without strife,

so finally,
we all can

breathe.

AlisRamie is from North Carolina, USA.
Interests include: philosophy, history, international relations,
poetry, art, design, jazz, funk, and some good old soul.
Allpoetry.com/AlisRamie

[Lisa F. Raines]

Your Kiss

You kissed me,
So soft and so sweet.

I miss you,
Still feeling your heat.

I listen,
For the fall of your feet.

Our tryst is
A beautiful retreat.

AlisRamie is from North Carolina, USA.
Interests include: philosophy, history, international relations,
poetry, art, design, jazz, funk, and some good old soul.
Allpoetry.com/AlisRamie

[Pamela Wyman]

Shade of Color

Green eyes smoke
ivory skin kissed by the sun
broad chest bare,
open land
to rest the auburn locks
of hair falling down around
a purity of bedroom eyes
in deepest brown

Ruby lips against pink skin
slides all flesh between ivory
doors, longing to lodge
longer in the bed of
crimson tongue

Blushing petals bloom
as sangria colors rush
through gray matter
floating clouds, white light
flash of thunderstorms,
cobalt oceans and sky-blue
all stream to become the
shade of color
known as us

Pamela Wyman is from Denver, Colorado and has been writing Poetry for 25 years. She humbly bows in submission as poetry writes the words that tumble from her mind to her pen, a partnership in ink. Allpoetry.com/Sweet_P

[Cory James Buchanan]

Fireless

I have not floated
still, lifting my head
from this dead ocean

opening like lightning
flashes, our Saviour
speaks in billows —
sunlight drops to
flattened water

a slamming ray
stalls me colourless;
blazing the horizon to
my eyes — heaven's
baron steps to me in
tides below thunder

survival is my rebirth,
blowing down an undertow,
grabbed to the torn
rim of this jupiter storm

my bare feet trail
cold red, treading
through biting gales,

within this hell
flooding fireless

––––––––––––––––––

Cory is from Winnipeg, Manitoba, Canada, and writes poetry as a therapeutic way to express himself. As well, he is 24 years old, and is continuing to practice writing poetry by self-teaching. Allpoetry.com/Coryjb

[Bob Buck]

Post-mortified

Gabardine suited Peyton.
The cloth of soupy sharkskin,
wanting pockets and lining,
secured his soulless rigor,
and clashed his peaky chin.

His silent sentimental snare,
depressed,
from lack of air,
but distressingly dressed,
and waisted thin,
gray paisley on pink pin,
disparately necked in charcoal,
Windsor knotted,
and pasted in.

Adjusted for display,
on a satinet sleigh,
formally dolled,
kenned and palled,
in undertaking play.

Jack,
a pretty man
with a pointed jaw
and lines tattooed

in between,
on the sides,
his fingers and hands,
kissed Peyt's
cold forehead.

Jump back!
A sweaty tongue!
A dribble!
A eye!
A cough!
A gasp!

Peyton,
shook his dead head awake,
once again.
Will the hairy harry ever end?
These self-conscious funs
in subconscious puns,
when will they stop?
After all,
what's dun is done.

———————————————

I am retired from data processing and counseling and I love
and live with my son's married family. Babies and music are
first and last orders of each day and the nurturing nature
muses some poetry. Allpoetry.com/bobbing

[Ronald S. Cohen]

Fishing in the Stream of Consciousness

gaze deeply into her blue eyes blue skies white clouds
floating about
white flowers bouquet white wedding dress her mother
sewed her
sunday morning down the aisle small church bells ringing
loudly
tinnitus the loud ring in my ear don't answer it says dr. kovac
funny guy retired in kansas writing books about space ships
maybe
self medicating mouth full of pills don't talk with your
mouth full
warns my mother my mouth drooling with sweet yellow
mango juice
mexican or the asian variety kind cannot remember which
mango
men go to war for no good reason come back with P.T.S.D
broken
S.T.D are sexually transmitted al capone evaded taxes for
years
was sent to prison could not save himself died there from
syphilis
see phyllis tonight it says in my calendar went on a date with
her
eating at the main course no corking charge what a bargain
bargain city went out of business was sold to a jewish
temple

shirley temple comes tap dancing along with those pretty curls

and cute dimples tap dancing the lost art of sammy david jr and

gregory haines heinz pickles are my favorites costco sells them

now together with car insurance proof of insurance $500 ticket

during a car accident not my fault though why the hell am i

apologizing to the reader let me just write this poem and be done

with it finally in the process using internal monologue stream of

consciousness freudian interpretations with no punctuation marks

inspired by the trend setter dorothy richardson and followed by

james joyce william faulkner albert camus sylvia platt virginia woolf

who is afraid of virginia woolf that big bad wolf not richard burton

or elizabeth taylor who are not afraid of her constantly abusive to

each other but i am the one afraid of virginia woolf and what she

started i dread to find out the real truth that no one dares to utter

that existentialism is like the nursery rhyme where life is but a dream or simply a metaphoric illusion that cannot be expressed

in words and therefore exists only in the mind of the beholder the
way that this so called poem exists only in the mind of this writer.

Born in 1947 in Cairo Egypt. Moved to Israel in 1949. Came to Los Angeles, California in 1963. Has an B.A , and M.a degrees in Judaic Studies and Literature from the University of California, Allpoetry.com/Ron_Cohen

[Essama Chiba]
A place of solitude

Crumbling away from the façade of pretense,
walking on a narrow strip of water,
listening to the sound of whirlwinds
echo on the island of gods,
clouds floating with silver wings
on top of Hydra skies.

Overviewing deep oceans,
through candlelit windows,
watching Athena sitting on the sill
playing the harp,
as the fishermen go out to sea,
to look at the moon and bring
back home the light of dawn.

Essama Chiba is a poet from Egypt who has been published
in a couple of Poetry Anthology's and co-authored several
poetry books of her own. She had a career in broadcasting.
Allpoetry.com/Essama_Chiba

[Radhika Lekshmi R. Nair]

baritone

silent swaying of the boat
soft breeze caresses the curls
soft whispers here and there
slanting sun was tired and worn

the evening ferry was sluggish
even as the passengers all
long hours of tedious haul
life is just about dragging on

his beard and hair tumbled unkempt
gypsy robes in vibrant colors
rustic face lined with time
bundle summed up chattel personal

amidst the boredom lulling the crowd
suddenly the gypsy broke out in song
words exotic, husky baritone
cobwebs cleared, the sparkle resumes

music tonic for souls and the minds
clearing lethargy dropping all wont
lightens the spirits soothing the senses
breezing away in colorful consensus

I am a doctor practicing medicine in Bahrain. I am a Keralite hailing from the southern most state in India. Started writing poetry since 2012. . Allpoetry.com/Gurupadam

[Radhika Lekshmi R. Nair]

Proud to be an Indian

India is my beautiful mother
missing you from miles away
across the seas of the Persian gulf
my heart pines for thy beautiful self

greenery covers you like a silk saree
beaches and the surf contrasts its borders
Himalay stands tall and elegant in the north
rivers are plenty garlanding you across

plains and valleys of rice, wheat and corn fields
swaying in the breeze, assenting valiant deeds
temples and mosques, churches and gurudwaras
never ending lines of rail spreading out like veins

Sanskrit mothering languages, took birth here, you see
Bollywood movies add glamour and masti for all to see
Tamil Malayalam Telugu Kannada Gujarati and Marati
Holi, Onam, Ganesh ulsav, Pongal, Dussera and Diwali

many a language and genre, many a taste and color
literature music and pictures tuning to the senses
united in our hearts we are, despite all diversity
"Janaganamana" with heads held high, proud of our rich
ancestry

Indian tricolor wraps us up in a cocoon of bright integrity
patience, non violence of Gandhiji, kohinoor of our national
identity
India is my country, and Indian, I am proud to be
India is my strong deep roots, wherever in the world I be..

———————————

I am a doctor practicing medicine in Bahrain. I am a Keralite
hailing from the southern most state in India. Started writing
poetry since 2012. . Allpoetry.com/Gurupadam

[Marcy Clark]
Beginner's Lessons

faith frays on a distant shore
and I struggle
chin deep in brackish riptides

my life jacket, once tethered on the dock
bobs past me on a drift of ash

and my breath bows in mildewed surf
wondering if I will drown
in hymns promising more rain

you murmur
and I breathe you in the wind,
feel the grit of shoreline
in a mourning dove's sigh

crawl through broken waves
to hug your roses in twilight
and drip shadows

in this new sea the dogs and I paddle,
knee-high splashes,
on the beach side of the shoal

I enjoy writing and volunteering in animal rescue-poetry exercises my mind and the critters bring me peace. Allpoetry.com/Grandmakittyfl

[Jack Mullen]

Niagara

Short the Niagara, swift.
"That current's too dangerous for swimmin'. "

Empties Lake Erie into Ontario
Ends in the great Falls, Marilyn Monroe did a movie there!

Before you git to the Falls is the largest freshwater island
I ever saw, maybe in the world.

Me and my dad and uncle hunted deer there long ago
Too many houses on Grand Island now.

We sailed a small sloop on the Niagara, a catamaran too
in the Sea Scouts—rowed a whaleboat pullin' altogether.

Grew up not far away, 'long the towpath
where they throw you in the Erie Canal to teach swimmin'

Yeah, that Niagara has a great current
you can see it—gets really worse near the Falls

But I swum it just up from Grand Island
walked back across the bridge

Nobody saw me, but I done it. Swam straight across
Hit the bank 'bout a quarter mile downstream

Never told nobody neither
Wouldn't 've believed me anyway.

———————————

Jack is from College Station, Texas where he is retired with Margie, his wife of 60 years, Retired from the Army and public school teaching, he spends his time with poetry and extended family. Allpoetry.com/Jack_Mullen

[Dakota Grinslade]
Moments Before Dying

this time you will learn
it hides its knives between
reality and my trust in all

nevermind the bullets
here's the new machine web

they'll be wiring our heads/necks
to covet our innermost visions

frigid zone secrets
spiralesque talk sick
wise clock counter
peeling away time

revenant wheels of regret
cut the circulation seer

ice skiver talisman
"Bite down on this!"

silent séance
stowaway inanimate me

grindstone facelift
notion-ripping currents

empty vessels fill the
belly of the whirlpool

dead, blue, violent ocean
state of emerge and see
in waves above

29y/o. Born and raised in Florida. Began studying music at age 11. Cello-'00, Guitar-'04, Bass-'09, Piano-'12. Writing began for me in '05 as a way to cope with losing loved ones who left too soon. Allpoetry.com/Dennis_Evahi

[Marta Green]

Sierra Mountains

our cabin is made of solid oak
smelling refreshing breezes
seeing deep snow banks

inside there are fur lined chairs
huddled around a crackling fire
with flames of red, orange and gold
warming cold bones, hands and faces

we have a dinner of Venison stew
roasting marshmallows over fireplace
next day we will go hiking
we pray the bears are still hibernating
at bed time, the moon glistens on the snow.

I have been married to my best friend for 10 years now who
makes me laugh to no end. My passions are family, animals,
especially writing, reading and art!
Allpoetry.com/Marta_Green

[Toni Lyons]

Old Man Winter

Old Man Winter has made his way to my town
wearing his robe made of snow and an icicle crown.
He opens his mouth and with a mighty roar,
spews blustery winds raging door to door.

Hands raised like a scepter to unleash his wrath,
a wintry mix blankets all in it's path.
From the snow covered hills to streets that are gleaming,
bare trees illuminate with icicles streaming.

Frozen crystal-like rain encasing my town,
old Winter has dressed us in a radiant gown.
Trimming the windows in a frosty lace,
for the finishing touches on this winter place.

As I step out and view this breathtaking beauty,
I realized old Winter had accomplished his duty.
A winter wonderland so quiet and serene,
sparkles and glistens, the perfect winter scene

I am from Huntington, West Virginia, now living on
Columbus Ohio for 17 years. I love writing because I can
articulate my thoughts and feelings more effectively than I
can verbally. Allpoetry.com/Talking_Toni

[James C. Allen]
First Time At The Beach

The skates at the beach swim in the ocean
like geese fly in formation.
Their skin wings and narrow tails propel
them.

In a moment they will in unison sail
just above the sea, still in a perfect V,
as if they might exercise an option to join
the geese.

Instead, they settle back into the water trough,
continuing the smooth propelling that is
silent and beautiful.

They vanish just before the waves cap,
but for black shadows cast against the
light sand of the floor, almost invisible
in their seamless and quiet liquid flight.

James is a poet reared in MS now living in GA. He is
designated, Fellow International Poetics Foundation. His
books are available through Amazon and Lulu.com
Founding member NOAIDS task force 1982.
Allpoetry.com/James_C._Allen

[Emily Brownlow]
can't unsee your eyes

tatty hummingbirds swarm inside demijohn skull
fiercely sipping sweet dregs of soured memories I cull
reaching high for sunrise behind freckled twilight
over skies whitewashed shy pours your arrogant night

hands swat dogged words from each uninspired ear
note gnarly wing snap mute a voice you won't hear
pinning lacklustre blots limp stains to my sleeves
memorial poetry ink freely bleeds

though I can't unlove you the cracks show I've tried
riding spent stars split the moon over-dried
I cannot unread you or unsee your eyes
I'll never un-fall
feels like dying   to try

_____

Emily nomiddlename Brownlow lives in the United
Kingdom in rural Norfolk. She loves to write poetry but is
not so keen on 'biographies'. Allpoetry.com/nomiddlename

[Carl Wayne Jent]
The Slow Walk

Poor chap
walking sadly
down dusty
trail
head hung low
spirits too
got up
after he
fell.

On his horse
left town
four hours
ago
leather saddle
six-shooter
rode off
slow.

Six-foot three
broad shoulders
every cowgirl's
dream
rode to ranch
meet his girl
getting lucky

seemed.

Off his horse
tie it up
walked in
tall
heard her
talking, moaning
down the
hall.

Peeked in door
eyes opened wide
face turned
red
drinking whiskey
two hired-hands
all naked
in bed.

She laughed
he cursed
fought men
lost
took his saddle
gun, girl
pride was the
cost.

Left worn

feeling small
looked like
hell
poor chap
walking sadly
down dusty
trail.

I've wrote poems for quite a while, the older I grow the more the poetry means to me. I hope the reader gets a little enjoyment reading my poems. Poems can open a mind and warm a heart. Allpoetry.com/Waynejent

[Pamela Wyman]

Dog Beach

Eyes wide as paws
rip open the
smooth liquid surface
legs quickly adapt
as water splashes
hot fur cools
a perfect smile
spreads across
his furry face
as he falls in love
with the lake
and wants to stay
ever summer day
chasing Frisbee's
in the cool water
at the Dog beach

Pamela Wyman is from Denver, Colorado and has been writing poetry for over 25 years. Pamela writes poems that represent a variety of genres from humor about her dogs or into the depths of death. Allpoetry.com/Sweet_P

[Jack Mullen]

The Difference?

We're Professionals, You See

Three hundred fifty miles
back and forth home college
rode my thumb back then

Mostly with truckers in tractor-trailers,
big rigs called 18 wheelers nowadays;
Knights of the open road we called 'em,
and we were right.

Like when outside Erie,
just after a Thanksgiving blizzard
we rolled over.

Four ruts in the snow down route 20
our only choice with the center two best
except when both directions were of the same mind;

Swerved out skidded, rolled over,
let down easy by a phone pole
that creased our hood as we stopped.

Yep, truckers showed up, found a rope,
pulled us back on our wheels,

lined us up in our proper ruts,
fist punched out the dented hood,
bent back the fan blade,
wouldn't accept when my ride offered a reward.

Lots of stories back then.
One told me of a sign on the dispatch bulletin board
"Remember, when you are out on the open road,
you are the professionals."

Ask any truck stop waitress who had the biggest hearts.

But, let me tell you my favorite:

"When we get to Toledo," he said,
"stick with me while I park this rig;
I'll drop you at a good spot to get you on your way."
He did. He parked. We got in his car, stopped for gas,
twenty-six cents a gallon if my mind is right.

He paid the attendant who handed him back some change.
"Put this in your pocket," he said, waving my protest away,
"Young man can always use money. Call it bread upon the
water."
(You gotta know, thirty-five cents an hour was good wages
dish-washin' then.)

He can never know as the years rolled by
(and gas got more expensive!)
how his voice raised up in the back of my mind

and the strange look in eyes now and then when I said,
"Forget about it. Call it bread upon the waters."

Knights Of the Open Road, The Professionals,
Our Truckers,
keep America moving local, down the open road,
made an indelible impression on a green college boy,
earned respect and honor with their deeds and code.

Jack is retired in College Station, Texas with his wife
Margie. They enjoy family outdoor activities with their four
children and 13 grand and great grandchildren.
Allpoetry.com/Jack_Mullen

[Eugene Michaels]

Emily

This ship has known many seas
embraced as stone all storms.
She can sense all hidden hazards
and needs no captain.

Past travels whisper upon these sails
her secrets safely stored below.
Let others plot with measure
maps made by these adventures.

Dear master, once commander
this craft will take no orders.
Her rudder is not broken
but guided from within.

Eugene Michaels pens poems while watching the deer, coyotes, raccoons, bobcats, squirrels, black bear, and the occasional mountain lion, scamper around the Sierra foothills of Northern California.
Allpoetry.com/Winterlove67

[Radhika Lekshmi R. Nair]

desert sands

SAND flows smoothly in the hour-glass of time
seconds gallop like a wild HORSE untame
clad in BLACK I wait for him to return
STORM brews in the skies to enthrall in turn

I am a prisoner of the HAREM esteem
enveloped in the SINUOUS draperies, I dream
my evenings clouded in UBIQUITOUS sheesha
I DANCE like a dainty nymph, my senses pita

mundane DISENTHRALL by magic wand
MUSIC of the HAREM harmonious band
behold the prince I always dream of, I squeal
as our eyes met, and the STORM was hard to conceal

night fermented in a saga of MUSIC and DANCE
JARS of wine emptied fast in reveling orgy, in a trance
tall swaying PALMS danced in silent witness
hot DESERT transformed into paradise par extravagance

dulling the senses, wine transfused in veins
glimpses faded blending dreams cellophane
dawn arrived in the SADDLE of exuberant feat
bleary curtains crushed in mysterious deceit

I am a doctor practicing medicine in Bahrain. I am a Keralite hailing from the southern most state in India. Started writing poetry since 2012. . Allpoetry.com/Gurupadam

[Carrie Mercedes Gogo]
Virgin Snow

landscapes once pivotal, now void of all life
Glistening diamonds, turn monochrome skis white

There is a rhythm; when snow falls and catches the eyes
Fragile and serene, untouched; natures blank canvas, perfect

The sounds of the season, hearing a newborn babies cry,
O stars amidst freshly fallen snow

Lanterns adorn cobblestone lanes, young lovers
hold on tightly as they leave footprints in the virgin snow.

Carrie Prieur was
Born in Historic Kingston, Ontario,
Canada 1975. Carrie's writing styles are free verse and prose.
Carrie hopes to publish a book of poetry in the future.
Allpoetry.com/SapphireRose

[Radhika Lekshmi R. Nair]

efforts to meditate

lights incense flowers water
mat folded hands sit still
close eyes deep breathe
settle down pray
concentrate
it's so hot
grocery list
mean neighbour
barking dog
concentrate
deep breathe
beautiful song
who's rung the bell?
concentrate
mind's play
children yell
musty smell
must do drill
chill make uphill
concentrate..
Rama Rama Rama...

I am a doctor practicing medicine in Bahrain. I am a Keralite hailing from the southern most state in India. Started writing poetry since 2012. . Allpoetry.com/Gurupadam

[Ayesha Ruqaiya Kashif]

Fine Wanderlust

Frozen Yellowstone.
A beauty unknown lends me
the crystalline faiths.

Thawing flakes, thawing heart.

A sordid shelter.
Whirlwinds of dust compassing
my down-trodden gates.

Built with agony.

Fiery souls engulfed
by the tempest urged to lead me;
Birthing chugging boats,
whom companion collapsing
white waters now fresh ashore.

Brewing feverish lust.

I trudge over bright fall leaves,
first seen among trees,
great stretches, magnificent like
blanched waves; my tsunami.

A clear storm with

distilled waters preying
on exploding pollen plumes
blooming night blossoms.

Lights drifting by my solitude.

Lanterns light the gloom.
Mother's cold womb snatched,
ripping sun's sinew.

Unleashed from the sky,
sun's course set anew.

The dry summer wind
whips weathering heather lays.
Bare bones, bitter sweat.

The toil of a thousand tears;
For worthy smiles resembling

welcoming foreign rains,
migrating like ocean currents
drowning many teacups of woes.
My fair-feathered life-long goals
experience continuous rebirthing.

I am born.

The mast is unbroken,
antique rusting, frosts fine touch.
Thousand-year vessel.

Sailing strong.

Seasons' limber touch.
Amber timber, melting kindle.
Suns eclipsing moons,
infinitely streaming stars,
everlasting wanderlust.

Ayesha is an avid traveler currently settled in Calgary,
Canada. She attempts to reflect this in addition to her
Pakistani roots through her work, and has been nominated
for various literary awards. Allpoetry.com/A._R._K.

[Nancy May]

From Now On

fried eggs -
crinkly grass!
pin the donkey -
frosty trees!
school bus

––––––––––––––––––

Nancy May has closed old dwelling holes. Nancy Asgard has taken over new dwells. Her new dwell can be found on Hiakuary. Her first collection is called Fledglings. Allpoetry.com/NancyAsgard

[Kyle Garon]

Breath Into the Grey

I walk under the silent morning,
greeted by ashy dark clouds.
A ferly midnight wolf
lays behind my eyes,
wondering if the blue vein tree
unveils in its dark heaven,
a howl erupts and shatters down.
Soaring down this road,
except I stray down somewhere else.
Following this callow
like curiosity I travel
further, I don't disobey.
Hints of ashen petals
sit inside my hollow tongue,
whispering to go back.
Weight of light
floods my whisp,
like a juice
from a woman's nectar.
Wanting to let my wolf free
as I lay in the ember leaves,
diving into the lake,
with one last howl enters
I fade.

Poetry has been a constant in the last eight years. I wouldn't know what else I would do. Poet for life.
Allpoetry.com/Lucious_Moon

[Marta Green]

Adventure, First Time Swimming

warm day in the Venezuela sunshine
excited and can't sit still
with my pink flip flops
wearing a matching swim suit

we are going to the public pool
holding my daddy's hand tight
he takes me and my siblings
to a little kiddy pool

my brother, sister and I
splash around in the cool waters
laughter like musical wind chimes
until there is a piercing scream

red water like a shark bite's victim
a little girl is lifted out of the pool
we are told to get out quickly
seeing a bloody foot, making prints

So scared yet fascinated
I had never seen so much blood
a mother had dropped a glass baby food jar
leaving the shards just waiting for a child.

daddy takes us to a big Olympic pool

taking turns jumping into my daddy's arms
from slate colored cement starting blocks
the scene from the kiddy pool forgotten

leaving the swimming area,
my daddy buys us some potato chips
from a street vendor, chips salty and crunchy
driving home, moutain jungles are seen in a distance.

I have been married to my best friend for 10 years who
makes me laugh to no end. My passions are family, animals,
especially writing, reading and art!
Allpoetry.com/Marta_Green

[David Donald White]

The Solstice and the Strawberry Moon

Her voice
made me shiver in the night
haunted by the longing in her song
Staring at billows of flame
erupting miles away
across a calm expanse
of black night and city light
A river runs through the darkness

Robins and blackbirds dart past
lakes and ponds beside the path
Feeling her presence
as she draws near

The full moon strawberry high
and bright in the solstice sky

The sun and his true love
dressed for each other
bright as they could
bright as they ever would
dancing in their day of light

Her melody louder now
come to life
She enters the stage

with milky fair skin
and messy red hair
flowing down in that Helios light
Oh, does that Sun God favor her

She sang in cooing crescendos
her wistful romantic idealism
whistling through every word

_____

David White is from Edmonton Alberta Canada. He writes
about his experiences with lost love and tries to capture the
beauty in pain and longing. He also goes by No-One and
The Young Red Shadow Dragon.
Allpoetry.com/DavidWhitePoetry

[Dennis Spilchuk]
Psalm 137:5—Not Forgotten

Psalm 137:5 If I forget you, O Jerusalem,
let my right hand forget its skill!
Psalm 137:6 Let my tongue stick to the roof of my mouth,
if I do not remember you,
if I do not set Jerusalem
above my highest joy! (ESV)

On May 14, 1948
The United Nations
Approved the proclamation
Declaring,
The "Independent State of Israel."

Seventy years later;
Monday, May, 14, 2018:
It is written in the history books;
"Oh Jerusalem, we did not forget you!"
Jerusalem is recognized
As the capital of Israel.
With the establishment of
The American Embassy
In the City of David;
By the 45th. President — Donald J. Trump,
Of the most powerful country
In the world.

The United States of America.

—————————————

I was born in Ontario, Canada and it is my hope that the poem 'Psalm 137:5--Not Forgotten' captures the enormity of the historical event that took place and will stand the test of time. Allpoetry.com/Denny747

[Lisa F. Raines]

Molting Trees

Spring trees bloom and petals fall,
new growth of brightly colored leaves
bursts forth from binding buds.

Summer's serene sun enriches
glorious deep green trees, storing energy
for the upcoming harvest.

Autumn's glowing trees shed
leaves of stunning splendor, falling softly
under heavy grey skies.

In winter's dreary dearth of light,
bare trees wait for the sun's rebirth.
New buds grow to bring back color.

AlisRamie is from North Carolina, USA.
Interests include: philosophy, history, international relations,
poetry, art, design, jazz, funk, and some good old soul.
Allpoetry.com/AlisRamie

[Marve Hendry]
back to black

my black sandals
felt the colours
  turn grey

summer came
  and ran away
 leaving trails
of burnt rubber
where once people laid content
contemplating the sun's tickling rays

  nights' blackness
matched only by days' rainbow sway

I finally surrendered
  my summer-wear
for autumn's tasteful black bra
and closed-footwear

———————————

Marve Hendry, aka Rhymedraven, is born from a feather and dipped into ponds of ice and fire. I write poetry for the fun of writing poetry, inspired by life events and injected with wild imagination. Allpoetry.com/Rhymedraven

[Carolyn Caudle Castle]
A Trip to the Valley

Students hope to see a river quite large,
Dreams built along the way build up a charge.
Cross the Rio Grande -
Dry as a bone.

Palm trees blow gently in a warm spring breeze.
Hombre strums a banjo as people slap their knees.
Flowers scent and colors of various sizes' –
Soothing and pleasant to tourists' eyes.

Open Market day, vendors all about
Price tag a starting point
Barter back and forth 'til both agree
Shoppers carry treasures home after quite a day!

Carolyn, is from the big state of Texas. My reason for living is Jesus, God's only Son, everyone's Saviour after death for eternity, if accepted so here... thus most of my poetry relates to Him. Allpoetry.com/CarolynCaudleCas

[Cj Crawford]

Texas Summer

It strips me of vitality
Fatigues me
Plaguing me with listlessness
It is a blazing, blistering heat upon my back.
Endlessly overhead and omnipotent
Unrelenting, mercilessly draining me
Ripping sleep from my faltering grasp,
I toss and turn in my bed, perspiration soaking sheets
Sole precipitation of saline
An unquenchable thirst wracks my palate;
leaves an intolerable taste.
I should have known from almanacs of amour passing as
seasons that perennials and durable prickly pines only
survive following spring in this state.
A perceived permanent pyre would cut the sky
Scorching and charring the creations of self given to you.

CJ Crawford is a queer poet living in Austin, Tx. This poem is inspired by Matthew Benavides, who's silent testimony of heartbreak inspired an understanding of a subject I never could approach alone. Allpoetry.com/PedanticDiocese

[Tine Sandmo]

The sun rises in your eyes

The brightest smile around
It still melts me to the ground
You bring laughter to everyone
Funny, stubborn, smart, strong, big heart
Before I met you I was falling apart

O sol nasce nos teus olhos
Tu trouxeste luz para minha vida
Tu completas-me
Nunca Nenhum outro coração conseguirá competir pelo meu
amor

In a new place
A new country
You brought another culture and language into my life
It is going slow but everyday I learn a little more
I want to know everything about the place that gave me you
The place that gave you to the world

Tu és o amor da minha vida
Sem ti, não haveria luz
O mundo não seria o mesmo
És uma bênção para todos nós

I am a 33 year old woman from Norway. I love writing poetry, it is therapy for the soul To me it is about describing my thoughts in a very real way.
Allpoetry.com/Norwegian_soul

[Uma Asopa]

Counting sheep

It
happened
to be a Tuesday
went like any other
day- hectic, nonchalant.
The evening was no relief
as it dragged like a novel with
no plot. I thought I could spend
the entire night looking at the ceiling
without blinking my eyes. Everything
around would desist from telling me its
magic lies –how the city slept on its loads
of worry, or the streets clutched on to pits of
hunger. How silence swept through the trees when
wind unleashed a chaotic temper. Dogs dozed lazily
breaking stillness with an occasional bark. Birds
became so quiet - did they lose their way in the
dark? Stars blinked intermittently giving away
some light. Did they all sleep at all, I don't
know - the sky has sealed the lips of the
night. It won't tell me a thing and I
know it won't help counting sheep.
A sleepless poet can only make
a pyramid of words. But if
I open these secrets
one by one, will

I fall off to
sleep ?

Poetry to me is way of reading into life with a deeper meaning , with a greater relish and sensitive eye. The reason is good enough to cmpel me to read and write poetry. I live in Ahmedabad, India. Allpoetry.com/Uma71

[Chanda Kaye Kolb]
Eternity

Those features faded into the stained glass of time,
following disfigured shadows
that glide across an afternoon horizon
A quiet crackle whispering secrets
through blades of Bermuda
while scents of lilac and musk dance
about a dew kissed morning
It's that slow burning ember
left from a blazing fire in your heart,
long after my dust has settled
into the grains of memory
My spirit is alive
within every heartbeat behind your smile,
catching any tear that dare fall from your eye
look into your reflection
and in memories
that were yours and mine
you are my eternity
where I will never die

For Brook, from Mommy 2001. My work is drawn from
pain, sorrow, joy, curiosity, and the simple quiet moments
we all experience. They are my thoughts, my questions, my
answers..
I am, I was, I will always be... me Allpoetry.com/sofargone

[Madeleine Mclaughlin]
She Told Me

about the wasting of days
and nights feeding lies to her mind
Powder like coffins set end to end
sucking broken bodies up her nose

but why
live in a suffering death house
or send your mind
to a dead end place?
why unravel the knitted
life of good things?
That, she couldn't tell me

Madeleine McLaughlin loves writing and swimming. Poetry is her relaxation from writing books and short stories. Allpoetry.com/celadia

[Andrew Blitman]

Stark

Day One:

Approaching a mountaintop,
The air is choked by snow.
Each labored breath wearies further
As the pressure dissipates with elevation.
Body heat emanates from the human body
Until the signature fully fades.

Day Two:

This ascension reaches a steep cliff
Jagged by rocks and icicle fragments.
My limbs are numb and stiff.
I cannot feel my fingers or toes.
A safe descent no longer seems feasible.

Day Three:

You have found the note in my resting place.
The avalanche must have been the summit's remark.

Take chances, but prepare first.

Stark

Andrew Blitman is a poet and artist who is also the webmaster of The Written Blit blog (www.andrewblitman.com). He is the published author of eight books, including the 'Wild Writers' series. Allpoetry.com/Andrew_Blitman

[Michael Thomas Hill]

Doomed Ship

DOOMED SHIP
Hurricane Sid swept the dead
Ship out to sea Patrick Sutton stood
On the seashore

Looked across the sea,
Saw a ship and whished
Farewell my love

He threw a penny down a well
The captain looked up at the tree
"What's this? A reflection of her

Who drowned in the sea?"
Whispering rain tapped on Patrick's
Windowpane,

Whispered in his ear
"Love isn't here.

Sheila stood on the deck of the ship:
She Whispered; "Goodbye, my love:

I'll wait for you at the gate of St Peter,
Where life's sweeter," She's young
As spring had been sprung

I like rock and roll music because this was around in the
year 1958: I was born on the 24th of February of that year.
The music would play on the radio in my childhood.
Would make mother mad that
Allpoetry.com/Michael_Thomas_H

[Rose Marie]

Chasing the Sun

Flying down a dirt road with the windows rolled down

Pushing the gas pedal to the floor

Throwing my hands up in the air as my hair blows

Smiling into the sunlight pouring through the window

Turning the country station up loud

Looking into the rearview mirror I see my self-grinning back

Singing along and dancing in my seat

Taking a quick turn and slamming into the door

Laughing so hard my stomach hurts

The fresh air filling my lungs

Stopping the old pickup and getting out to dance on the soil

The breeze pushing and pulling my body

Closing my eyes wishing for this moment to never end

Jumping up onto the tailgate and letting out a scream

Letting everything out

Slapping a hand onto the hood I jump back onto the ground

Climbing back into the truck, putting it into drive, slamming

on the gas pedal, and flying off down the road

I am from Iowa. I write poetry as a way to express myself. When I write poetry I feel like I have found my place in this world. Thank you for reading. Allpoetry.com/Rose1059

[Ayesha Ruqaiya Kashif]

Movement for Justice

Our secular state;
A consideration strictly woven and cast
effortlessly by his hands.
    A timid cape
    enveloping us.
    Our deprived namesakes.
Bright embers, kindling rigid strokes of his pen.
Words flowing like blood drawn by
our un-partitioned states.

Our vessels rubbed dry.
Empty.
Reset with rejoice,
a foreign feeling,
for a distant haven, ours to compose,
A freedom to choose.
    A freedom to live.
Carved by tears into stone.

And we changed,
rupees to annas
    converted to rupees once more.
And we changed.

The coveted affairs
of the new state,

harsh like summer monsoons.
Their sweet rain churning,
The brine that bore the birth of our streets.

An acidic state.
Sanded waters swiftly
      Eroding. Corroding.
      Shattering stone.

      Cataclysmic.

And like his words, his blood pooled
in our flooded, hastily-paved ways.

A state now sovereign
from his considerations,
Which remain

      forgotten.

Ayesha is an avid traveler currently settled in Calgary,
Canada. She attempts to reflect this in addition to her
Pakistani roots through her work, and has been nominated
for various literary awards. Allpoetry.com/A._R._K.

[Zhao Lun Ma]

He is in the bath

Lost in the path
Strange, also no end.
I could not find a way
Out but only followed the passage
Into the deep woods.
Staying still by the stone
The roots surround
With no more space.
After fifteen minutes, not long,
One creature walked out
Vulnerable and stealthy.
With eight legs
A small body and belly
He choose not to jump away
Only stillness - no sound, no motion.
He made up his mind
Walked close to my thigh
Climbed up there calmly
Cleaned himself with help
From his legs.
It did not bother him
I handed him some dew from the foliage
Into his hands.
I only wished to so
He could have a nice

Bath,
The tiny spider.

I don't have a particular purpose in life. Some times I drink coffee at the coffeshop. Some moments I stay at home and spend time with family. Most times I like to see what happens in the natural world through the internet. Allpoetry.com/Clark_Ryan

[Kelli Ellis]

Empty

Through bloodshot eyes she stares into the mirror
An empty corpse of a woman.
You can see it in her eyes,
She wants to be ok
But she's not.
Her eyes were once filled with hope and wonder,
Like an evergreen forest waiting to be discovered.
Whenever she met him
She was set on fire.
It started off as a small spark
Then turned into a forest fire.
Slowly shell be ok,
For she will grow her forest back.
This time guarded,
With a wall so tall
Only the willing can come in.
Someone who will water her trees,
Not burn them down.

––––––––––––––––––

Kelli Ellis is a 20 year old college student from Whitehouse,
Tx that enjoys writing poetry in her spare time.
Allpoetry.com/Summerpower27

[Candy Campbell]

A day I'll never forget

We visited the riverbank on a hot summer day in my t-shirt wading in the water we play.

Walking hand-in-hand we laughed giggled and splashed, walking as we feel the mud squished between our toes, that is a day I'll never forget.

As we went around the corner to the waterfall I picked up some rocks all shapes big and small.

Tossing rocks in, you show me a trick, like a little kid I watched in awe as the rock went across the crick.

Laughing at what I accomplished I was happy as can be. The day that we visit the riverbank is a day that I'll never forget.

Dedicated to my one true love, Good Looking. I am so glad you found me. I am blessed to have you by my side. Thank you for loving me and being the inspiration for my writings. I love you always. xoxox Allpoetry.com/Candycane12977

[Ayesha Ruqaiya Kashif]
Hooks & Lanterns

Raging flood of time, seconds frothing, overwhelming
While she's leaning back, keenly watching Snow Paragons
listlessly

Mend, Melt, End

Snow pools into the craters, forming lakes, and her way's
left

Lost, Crossed, Untended

But the Lake's Veiled.
The soft glow of lanterns too far off in the distance.
Can't she see? She can't see

What all the other girls know
While all the other ones know.

Instead she's suffocating.
On paper lanterns dimming, sinking deep into the melt.
But she sees them floating up, into foreign sky, hopeful and
bright.
Only 'cause she's upturned, head first, in the lake drowning.

Struggling, scratching towards the Violin High Rise midst
bright teal snow slough
Others fish her out with golden treble hooks, see her heart's *l*
shaped.

Yet they try to force her through an *f* shaped hole,
And quietly she listens.

To the Festering Sounds, of the septic hounds, that surround,
                                        All disguised as people.

And she braves it all
        All unknowingly, strains her heart to be an *f* shape.

Then it's near nine
        And the hounds've strung her up on a fishing line
        Reeling her till she's near the ninth

Floor.
        Finally, She looks down
                To the old crater, the now renewed lake.

    Puzzled eyes watching the old melt slowly ice over now
                Yet lanterns are still splicing in deeply somehow
                As if they're a fragment of the snow's DNA now
                        All her bright lanterns are lost to a pit.

She knows,
                She was only a pawn

She can't believe she'd thought she'd be fine.
        Just playing puppet for the brave old dawn.

As the night hits, she hears a crow, against the tower a

leering shadow shows

> Between them a failed mirror
> She's a false reflection it jeers

Then the last clock ticks. The last minute ticks. The frothing
seconds smoothen to a
stop.

And she lets go, cutting the line, falling to the snowy depths
below.
Time is renewed.

Now she passes a lonely one, tattered, worn by time.
> She wonders if he's in her past phase
> > But lets her heart sweep past his silent gaze.

> When she's past, pats for change.
> > Her eyes slightly shifting with a guilty look.
> > > In the end she's still caught on those treble hooks.

Ayesha is an avid traveler currently settled in Calgary,
Canada. She attempts to reflect this in addition to her
Pakistani roots through her work, and has been nominated
for various literary awards. Allpoetry.com/A._R._K.

[Michael Bradley]
Temporary Bones

A snapshot
in Time.
Glossy pages, bursting at the seams,
overrun by those
we love and
despise.
Lines of women are deprived of basic human rights;
starving with a hunger only to be satisfied by abuse;
and made to sit still,
for she who takes the front cover
doesn't move.
They were all once girls -
daughters -
and had aspirations like you and I,
yet heavy linen
and soft silk
tie at the legs, and
comfort becomes
confinement.

Wrapped in a simple aesthetic,
purportedly summoned by a group of scientists
with less sense of la mode
than a vagabond,
who at least gets a glimpse
of the happening streets,

fuchsia, navy blue and alizarin crimson
allure the senses,
heightened for a reward for
following the fastest needleworker.
The brighter the hue,
the more blinding.
Overseeing the world's
demand
for greedy taste buds.
"Cave" leaves the dripping tongue.

Bigger and better.
Black is white, yellow is a shape,
life is simultaneously nothing
and every
thing
in a world of nothing.
Tugging at mother's Chanel fleece,
a hungry mouth asks
why
he has more than a man 4 times
his age.
Ignoring the fashion,
with an eavesdrop,
that grizzly figure engages:
"Son, your mummy walks behind
the shadow of skeletons,
bone white cotton hiding their withering.
That's not everything.
Bones are what you and I have,

and though the weather
is unkind to my own,
they let me go
outside of a straight line
some may call a Cat Walk.
Designers don't make bones,
they break them."

In my early 20s. Northern Australia. An obscure perspective
and a desire to express it. Heavily influenced by poetry in
music, and Spanish literature. Allpoetry.com/Miguel-

[Michael Donald Gustin]

Respect

I'm Respected but its because I'm repeatable.

Dude I even hid your needle.

I got sent home, not you, so fuck you.

Got sick with the aquana flu.

So give me my respect.

I tried to change your perspective on this thing.

But you continued to try to fuck me over.

Did you hear the ding when they rang that bell.

How about them jets straight from Dover.

I didn't know you wanted to be in hell.

Black horse, black mask.

Fuck you and your dad.

Most of you aren't shit but white trash.

See your forehead when you get in a crash.

For-knowledge of me sitting back laughing drinking a martini.

Where's my part of the margin.

Not trying to charge in just want my piece of the pie.

Pinky finger towards the sky.

I write because this is my life.

Ok babe.

Skypoet originally born and raised in Seaford DE. Lived in parts of North Carolina and Maryland also. Wasn't the most respected child or adult until the middle of this year. Pushed, beatened, bullied! Allpoetry.com/Skypoet_1816

[Kelly Frederick]

Fashioned

Silken black dawn soon
One eclipsing sun loom
A spindle lock bloom

Have been trying to leave some of myself, and perception
for others to contemplate with criticism.
So I will continually grow with eventual wisdom.
Allpoetry.com/Saplingtree9

[Daniel P. Quinn]

Kept Coming Back

Pillbox, black top.
Maybe I'll take two.
Covered one eye while playing hopscotch.
To see the silhouettes you drew.
You pulled my hand down,
Towards the ground.
Just to get a better view.
Made me believe you'd care,
And I was meant to fall in love with you.
Came here on a whim.
To only leave in a hurry.
Prayed to him.
Was a slave to him.
The pain we had to bury.
Walked the line.
While waiting for a sign.
Looked through window & door.
Was hopeless...
But I kept coming back for more.

I always have used poetry to express how I feel. Have been writing for 15 years. Hope you like this one.
Allpoetry.com/Sabibdd

[Avinash Jalani]

Finding blueprint

Sun is sleeping on the leaves,
Mountains staying by the lakes,
Mother caressing her child,
Traveller chasing their dreams.

People pushing each other for a win,
Success coming at a cost,
An empty eyes all round dinner table,
Losing in their own search.

Reaching the destination,
Filling eyes with more rivers,
Heart scared at the night light,
Searching for a shelter.

Arriving at the door with no walls,
Opening the door with no choice,
One foot stepping on the snow,
Another resting on the grass.

Seeing multi-universes with one mind,
One cold another warm with ears burning,
Realising this self-creation,
Moving forward one step at a time in surrender.

Avinash Jalani who is settled in Australia started writing to connect with this universe through self-healing. His poems are resonated during moments of self-reflection, struggle and stillness.
Allpoetry.com/Treedream84

[Paul Goetzinger]

The Bookstore

There's something about a bookstore
It's where you go
It's a library, a gathering spot, a refuge, a journey
It's crowded with people
Elaborating loudly about the smell of books
Some like vanilla, others like almond or coffee
Always books
Books stacked to the ceiling

It's a magical place
Endless shelves of stories and characters
Customers standing rigid in front of the proper section
Employees wandering the aisles
Neatening up the books
Standing alone, scouring shelves with hungry eyes
Keeping bookcases stocked
Carrying around stacks
Caressing worn books with cracked spines
Sauntering upstairs to the magazine racks
Removing aisle sitters, fixated on a particularly scary
passage
From a famous horror writer
Stopping by the reading chairs
Asking multiple times if you need help
Priding themselves on their knowledge of their assigned
sections

Peaking their passive aggressive phase, while working at a
bookstore

The kid's books are located at the back of the store
A catchall section full of ambiguous titles
Where stories begin with "In the beginning" or "Once upon
a time" or "It was love at first sight"
A section full of games, puzzles, teddy bears and throw rugs
Giving off the sour tang of a picked over flea market

The bookstore is serendipity
Walk in and your world falls away
Just you and the books
Pockets of words and paper that transports you to a different
place
A mix of the young and the eccentric
College students and lifers
A place for grazing the written word
In wide open spaces
While a lonely security guard stands watch
Just hired after a shoplifting incident

Books
Lined up in open cases
Spread out on tables
Highlighted on platforms
Displayed on 5-foot high wire racks
Thronged masses filling the checkout counter
Looking for obscure philosophy texts
And up to date computer manuals

Books have an aura
An excitement about them
You can tell by the way people look at them
Touch them
The way it feels in their hands
While they walk upwards floor by floor
With improvised book marks still in them
Waiting for the crowd to disperse
So they can purchase their dreams

Paul Goetzinger is an educator and writer from Des Moines, Washington. He uses poetry to inspire and mentor his students. Allpoetry.com/Paul_Goetzinger

[Andrew Lee Joyner]

Th6 m|nd of a tWiz+ed souL

Tossing and turning, infinite thoughts
Racing in circles, like a spider's web,
branching off in all different ways
N0 straight li~~ne, no idea that stays,
m0Re cON+!nue tO chAng6 aLl tHe time
Posz!bLy youR's, MosT l|k6ly mine_
c0NfuZ!ng, DIS+URBED, spiral|ng Down

Weird yet DIFFERENT, L1kE An InSaNe clowN

A// These thoughts Build Up !Nsid6

_____

When i started writing it became a hobby of mine and now
in the long run It's become a goal . I love to read and write;
my inspiration comes from events i may encounter.
Allpoetry.com/Andrew_lee

[Ayesha Ruqaiya Kashif]

Boreal Winds

Under the lull of the winter sun I remembered you.
A bright face once smiling.
Hair plastered to a little crown caught midst snow dunes.
Your laughter, sweet kindle for boreal winds,
calming my misgivings. A solitary moment
encompassing a solid heartbeat.
Smothering me, engulfing me.

The past heart's gifts to the present.

On the gravel beaches of White Rock
we stood. Fixed as one being,
where the great humpback once lay.
Wisps of ocean spray
lapping the tips of our toes. Yet
we stood steadfast. Your young heart shielding us
from the fierce sea weather
cutting and ripping our hopes,
pulsating in the unknown.
And from the rifts of a gentle breeze
you ignited into a whirling gale,
culling drifting rabbles.

Between us, a brief affinity had formed,
The shade cast by freckles of snow.
A warm shadow drawing you and I together.

Enabling you to release the source of
your laughter. My late joy. Your nightingale.
Akin to fleeting dreams;
Stark silhouettes in a foreign horizon.
Soaring with arrogance,
embracing a burning blizzard of birds.

Then from my depths you found doubt's hand crawling.
Clandestine words lasting only one sentence
– Worth half my lifetime; you.

The past heart lost to the present.

Your body writhed under my weight.
A flaming heat now turned to ember,
gagging on my sordid thoughts.

The nightingale's wings lifted, beating
helplessly in my tempest.

Ayesha is an avid traveler currently settled in Calgary,
Canada. She attempts to reflect this in addition to her
Pakistani roots through her work, and has been nominated
for various literary awards. Allpoetry.com/A._R._K.

[Lisa F. Raines]

Often I Tire

Often I tire,
here by the fire,
Listening to the mire
reported over the wire.

We wonder and look higher,
Aspire to a spire,
listening to a choir;
Is that a lyre or a liar?
A prior or a pryer?

Much of what we require
Is what the entire shire desires
Not your ire, nor a pyre,
Just a plea to live long and retire.

AlisRamie is from North Carolina, USA.
Interests include: philosophy, history, international relations,
poetry, art, design, jazz, funk, and some good old soul.
Allpoetry.com/AlisRamie

[Lisa F. Raines]

Little Lily

Lovely, lovely,
literary language
listening lovingly to
Little Lily laying
Lightly in the lady's lap.

Inspired by Brundaban-panda. AlisRamie is from North
Carolina, USA.
Interests include: philosophy, history, international relations,
poetry, art, design, jazz, funk, and some good old soul.
Allpoetry.com/AlisRamie

[Julie Radford]

A long Winter

A long, long, winter this has been.
The sun is welcome, but does not a thing.
Cracking sounds everywhere, from the snow-covered carpet,
most everywhere.
Hunger, it drives me, no food can be seen,
The stores I had built, the cupboards are clean.
Heavy in debt, and payment is due.
I must find food, before daylight leaves too.

In the distance, a vixen cries, she is hungry, and I'm her
prize.
Edge of the forest, temptation grows, the sun beats down,
onto a small meadow.
In the centre, fresh grass grows, Spring is close, and danger
knows.
To venture further, a vixen knows, a banquet awaits an
unwary foe.

A choice must be made, cruel, and uncaring.
Do I go forward, where a vixen is waiting?
Stay in the forest, where safety surrounds me.
A debt must be paid, or hunger will get me.

Stepping forward, a choice is made.
The vixen spots me, and plays her game.
The grass is sweet, and a welcome treat.

I made a mistake, when I see her leap.
Nowhere to run, nowhere to hide, this is it, my time is now.

In the distance, a flash of light.
A noise, it shakes my very mind.
The vixen, falls by my side.
And I run to the forest, with a meal inside.
Dear vixen, who was hungry too.
Who was the target, me, or you?

———————————————

I live with two boys, and two dogs, Tizer, and Pepsi, why
the name Tizermax. I live in the UK, near Sherwood Forest,
and the legends of Robin Hood. My mind races with stories,
and poems. Allpoetry.com/Tizermax

[James Cameron Melahn]

When I See

When I see
a hot pink sunrise,
I think of a purple night sky.
When I see
a colorful rainbow,
or all the blooming flowers in a row.
When I see
a lusciously red rose,
I am glad you are
the one my heart chose.

As a young child I can still remember playing out side in the fields in my neighborhood. When it was time to come home I would go to my room and write. Writing has always been a passion of mine. Allpoetry.com/Raiders0725

[Lisa F. Raines]

Anger

Anger animating
my every move,

With a thrust and parry,
of every groove,

until I've been hurt, and
hurt enough to prove,

how friction does not behoove
the strength of our smooth interlude.

AlisRamie is from North Carolina, USA.
Interests include: philosophy, history, international relations,
poetry, art, design, jazz, funk, and some good old soul.
Allpoetry.com/AlisRamie

[Patricia Marie Batteate]

Unhappy Trails

Spontaneous combustion
Blood flows to the head
Adrenaline released
Eyes see red

Strike without mercy
Reflex action
Deployment of words
A mutual transaction

Heart pumping fast
Sweat soaked shirt
Hostile contact
A scrap in the dirt

Accusation exchange
Hearsay no doubt
Ego's challenged
A boasting of clout

A blow to the nose
Blood starts to flow
Respect is lost
They've stooped that low

Headlock dispatched

Nowhere to go
Requesting "uncle"
Reply with a no

Chemtrails all day
Victims of fallout
People are enraged
But they don't know what about

I am a 8th generation Californian. I am an engineer, poet
and artist. I could see poets inheriting the earth.

Allpoetry.com/Patricia_Marie

[Lynn Dowless]
Johnny Dollar Do This And That

Johnny Dollar had some doe.
Johnny Dollar sang all day
while he worked and cleaned the floor.

Johnny Dollar load my hay.
Johnny Dollar do some more,
since you love to get your pay!

Johnny Dollar take me there.
Johnny Dollar bring me here.
Johnny Dollar take me where
I may clip my nails and cut my hair,
then drop me off to get my beer!

Oh Johnny Dollar take me far.
Oh Johnny Dollar clean my yard!
Drop me off at aunt Sadie's car;
hope that I don't come down too hard.

Johnny Dollar fetch my wine,
then find the family a place to dine.
Should you find that your day is through,
then come to me for more to do!

Never worry because you will be paid well.
I have lots of scrap for you to sell.
I have lots of paint for you to brush,
so your complaints you may then flush.

Johnny Dollar here are my keys.
There is my house, so do as you please.
Wash my dog and cut my grass,
pick up pecans and shine my glass!

Oh Johnny Dollar May comes soon,
time for plowing and party balloons.
You'll have fun and you'll be fed,
because here is where the King's daughter will be wed.

Oh Johnny Dollar where are you now?
Go fetch our brush and find our cow.
Go find Uncle Bill and Sister Sue,
because she told me that she is the one for you!

Oh Johnny Dollar May comes soon,
she'll be your bride and you her groom.
She'll mend your cloth and cook your food,
and you'll fix her car and cut her wood.

So Johnny Dollar here's some more,
go feed the sheep and fix our floor.
Go butcher the calf and hang the moon,
because the days pass fast and May comes soon!

Johnny Dollar we are so proud!
You stand so tall above the crowd.
We'll all have shelter and plenty to eat.
You'll always have a stash of money and friends to greet,
since you have a determination that can't be beat.

Oh Johnny Dollar where are you?
Without your presence we are so blue.
Without your cash we are in harms way,
our growling bellies will have their say.

So Johnny Dollar come back soon!
You hung the stars, so do the moon.
You pay our bills and give us thrills.
You work all day since you are so hardy,
so that you may be the life of the King's party.
So Johnny Dollar shoe shine too..
Oh Johnny Dollar where are you?

The author is an international ESL instructor. He has been a
writer for over thirty years. His latest published title is
'Once Upon A Time In Nottoway,' . He enjoys meeting his
loyal fans. Allpoetry.com/Poetry180

[Jasmine Galiste]

I Am a Puppet on Strings

I want to be free
for once in my life
I want to be happy
without paying a price

There is so much
that I've given up
I look at myself
and I feel corrupt

I want to say
so many things
but when I'm with you
I'm a puppet on strings

I am an actor
reciting my lines
assuring myself
it'll all be fine

I am a bird
trapped in a cage
slowly boiling
with more and more rage

You look at me

but what do you see?
Am I who
I'm supposed to be?

Jasmine Galiste from Sacramento, CA, poetry helps me straighten my mind out and make sense of the world that surrounds me. Allpoetry.com/Reese_Collins

[Claire O Dwyer]
Behind all emotions

Deep down life is through. Now your hiding the real you.

Life is holding all you need but mind and body cannot see.
Today tommorow is a distant regret thinking nothing can do
you help.

Behind your eyes you see the faith a wonderous future does
await. Rite now you can't see this to be true, raise your chin
and let faith through.

Today tommorow and rite now life can change wherever you
are. Hold onto all you know but let that darkness and pain
go.

It is nothing to you now no grieve no hurt can drag you
down. Stand up and feel that faith and something amazing
will remain in place.

Claire O Dwyer from Ireland. Poetry is raw and very
meaningful to me to express feelings and hopefully help
others. Allpoetry.com/Claireod

[Joanne Zylstra]

Sitting in a Chair

Sitting in a chair next to her bed,
The silence was calming,
It wrapped me in warmth,
But this leads me to despair,
As I touch her silver hair.

Watching her sleep,
Hoping she is lost in a dream-world
Of all her fond memories.

A moment later she awakes,
The burning - she is crying,
The burning - she is sobbing,
Watching her face makes my heart ache.

Day after day,
The pain never goes away
So many pills.

I love her so much it makes me mad
Feeling so stressed,
Wishing her sleep would overcome
Not knowing the outcome of the life she now leads.

Some of us who are blessed
Forget to be thankful,

But somehow she keeps her faith
Through all the pain and anguish.

There is pain and sadness
Watching her struggle,
But I hope there's an end
To put her at rest

———————————————

Married since 1984 to my husband, Tom and we have two children, Andrew and Allison that amaze us everyday. Allpoetry.com/Mommy_Bear

[Margarita Konova]

Captivated

Vivid blue eyes and flaming hair,
she awaits in the mist singing the song.
Sweet glossy lips and dulcet tones
lure him into a miracle of soft splendor and wondrous
enchantment.

Like a sea siren, unattainable and fascinating,
a vision so delicate and iridescent,
her presence engulfing his senses
leaving him gasping slowly for breath.

Beguiled by her fair charm
he steps into her heavenly realm
so entranced by her diamond beaded skin,
longing for her silky touch, for the passion that is hidden
deep within her.

She sits alone, so dignified and yet so frail
her gaze upon the crashing waves
a sign of sorrow and yet so much love
embedded in her regal frame.

His heart beats fast...
What if she is a dream?
How is it possible for such perfection
to not exist, to not be real?

She slowly fades away,
her angel voice dying in this quiet day.
Captivated by her graceful smile,
so transfixed he reaches out,
but it's too late... she's gone...
Only shadows left to remind him
of her alluring beauty.

I am originally from Bulgaria currently living in US. Poetry helps me cope with days when I feel lonely. It also helps me express my feelings when I feel happy. In my spare time I love to travel. Allpoetry.com/mkbg

[Andrew Lee Joyner]

Magic

A life force
Not all about tricks and games
It is a source of energy
Unnoticed by most
The balance between all emotions
All around the world

Not just cosmic energy, but a light
It shines brighter than the sun,
Cannot be seen, but can be felt

We all have magic in us
All you have to do is look
Deep within your heart and soul
There is your own different kind, of energy

Energy are like auras
Different colors and shades
It all comes from magic

Both light and dark
It is our choice to give into either path
Our choices are just another form of magic

In the end it's all magic

When i started writing it became a hobby of mine and now in the long run It's become a goal . I love to read and write; my inspiration comes from events i may encounter. Allpoetry.com/Andrew_lee

[Ruth Hodgins]

The Cry Of Camelot

Arthur, oh Arthur, can't you wake somehow?
Camelot has fallen, you're the only one left now
My Great King, your widow calls to you
Hear her dying screams from beyond the great blue
Mordred has taken over, Morgana at his side
Merlin cannot be found, nothing is turning the tide

Where then is Excalibur, if you will not wake this day
We need something to give us the chance to steal away
Can't you see that your Round Table is in ruins
The Knights cannot hold off all these evil Druids.
The records and the wizard said you would return
When Camelot needed you most, but now your kingdom
burns

Can you not hear the screams of this falling city?
Can you not see our once-enemy's hearts now full of pity?
My lord, Camelot needs her king.
If you cannot do this, put the sword back in the ring
Back in the ring inscribed on magic stone
Back so we can find a worthy heir to the throne

You must see something where you are
Camelot has never fallen quite so far
This noble spire once stood for good and peace
Now it's a reminder that our enemies we must please.

Queen Guinevere lies in a tomb beyond the hill
She died of grief before she could be killed
Knight Lancelot is now just a drunken failure
Cannot even lift his sword to drive off his jailer
The once Great Knights are now no more,
The Round Table is ruined in a room with a shattered door
They keep saying you are coming, magic does exist
Why then are you not here, appearing from the mist?

Arthur, now Camelot needs her King
Do you hear, you are our only capable thing
The Great City of Camelot has fallen
Don't you know that now your people are in coffins

You once told stories of how Paradise was fair
Of how it could never even compare
To how much you loved your realm
Your love for us would always overwhelm
Every tug at your heart just to stay
In Avalon, that sweet paradise so very far away

But now we watch as Camelot falls,
Are you even hearing our calls
Great King Arthur, where in Avalon are you now
Is Paradise really worth the destruction of your crown?

Ruth is a 19 year old poet from North Carolina. Poetry became an outlet for her after two of her high school teachers inspired her to just keep writing, no matter what was going on around her. For H&R
Allpoetry.com/Beginning_Again

[Dominic Houlihan]

hourglass

To walk among the street where once you came to see so
many new faces how so much has time changed.

As time goes by like a hourglass
part of wishes you can go back.
To treasure those moments that we once had lost.

Friendly banter
the smiling neighbours
the old stock storys
O how time has changed.

As or time on earth comes to an end.
I hope i leave enough story's to tell for all my family and
friends.
to leave a legacy that my name will always remain...

Dominic Houlihan is from Co Kerry Ireland I started using
poetry to help me express myself through my pen
Allpoetry.com/Dominichoulihan

[Justin Chang]

seasons of change

listen,
the seasons beckon you.

the warmth of the sun,
the touch of the warm rays,
the scene of a crisp, blue sky.
reminding you how admirable your life is.

the pouring rain,
bashing on your roof and windows.
but if you listen closely
it's as if someone is clapping for you.
Praising your heroic efforts in a period of hardship.

the white snow.
the grace of white in the lethal white dagger.

listen... for they reflect the trials and blessings that we
receive.

Justin Chang is a poet who has been writing since 7th grade.
and with encouragement from parents and teachers, he
decided to make his poetry public to not only be realistic,
but comforting. Allpoetry.com/freeverse254

[Lisa A. Hamilton]

Comfortably Numb

Little black heart of mine
scarred, cold, and empty.
How deep does your darkness go?
How do you keep beating like you do?
How is it, that love still flows from you?
Giving love chance after chance, after all you've lost and
been through.
I wonder...will you ever be the same as you were so long
ago?
My little black heart laughed and said
"Probably not, but it's worth a shot.
After all, it's just another bullet hole."

_____

Lisa A. Hamilton is a passionate, fun, and loving Mother and
Grandmother from Galax Virginia who has a desire to spill
poetry from her soul in her spare time.
Allpoetry.com/Lisa_A._Hamilton

[Dominic Houlihan]

Father's love

I sit alone again at night always thinking of you.
Your the first thing on my mind when I wake and the last
thing at night.

Holding you for the first time I felt my life was so complete.
With eyes like the ocean.
My tears ran ever so deep.
From your cheeky little smile and your beautiful laugh.
You know you had me right in the pam of your hand.

As I count down each and every day so I can see you.
Because whenever where apart I hope you never forget you
will always have a huge piece of my heart.

Dominic Houlihan is from Co Kerry Ireland. Poetry is one
of the best ways to feel and get so much emotions across
through your pen Allpoetry.com/Dominichoulihan

[Haylee Michelle]

Mia Ann

Just yesterday we heard your heartbeat,
This moment is bittersweet.
With just days that remain,
Excitement so hard to contain.

Room perfectly put together,
Clothes ready to wear.
Puppy is ready,
The preparation for your arrival finally at an end.

Your body grew still,
Worries began to overfill.
Our tears flowing fast,
Learning that our baby has past.

How could this be,
You were just so healthy,
This was not part of our plan,
But you will always be our Mia Ann.

Haylee is 23, from Arizona. Writing has been a love of mine since I was little to have an outlet during tough times. My life revolves around being a role model for my sisters and make my grandma proud. Allpoetry.com/HayleeMichelle

[Dylan Bennett]

Last dose

Here's a toast.
To one more dose.

Maybe this one will be my last.
Though two more would be a blast.

I just need to up my take.
I'm sure it will not be a mistake.
I may invite you to my wake.

So raise a glass.
To my past.

But this time will be my number.
As I lay down for one final slumber.

―――――――――――――

A railroad worker and proud father, I was born in Central Pennsylvania in 1994. Born with a rare deficiency that involved several surgeries in my youth; I find solace in my writing. Allpoetry.com/Crow88

[Lisa F. Raines]

Mockingbird Haiku

A mockingbird sings
his ever-fresh repertoire;
I strain to hear him.

His soliloquy,
lilting and warbling, in turn,
calms my wearied mind.

Daytime nightingale,
he interprets surrounding
sounds gloriously.

Hearing him moves me
toward contentment
as nothing else does.

AlisRamie is from North Carolina, USA.
Interests include: philosophy, history, international relations,
poetry, art, design, jazz, funk, and some good old soul.
Allpoetry.com/AlisRamie

[Lisa F. Raines]

A Primer in Profundity

Punditry
Plundering

Perfunctorily
Purposeful

Permutations of
Pioneering

Presidential
Propaganda --

Portending a
Preamble to

Present
Potentiality, and

Possible
Probability --

Promising
Projections

Professing
Protectionism, and

Preserving
Power --

Pending
Problems

Predicted by
Prescient

Public
Protestation.

AlisRamie is from North Carolina, USA.
Interests include: philosophy, history, international relations, poetry, art, design, jazz, funk, and some good old soul.
Allpoetry.com/AlisRamie

[Joanne Zylstra]

Arms Are Open

Arms are open my dear child,
Gates are ajar for your sweet entry,
Ready to welcome you by my side.

The angels dwell with you unseen,
with every thought, every word and every action
you've given your heart like a vase for thy flowers

Your heart is white
like the wings of angles' that watched
you pray every night

I've heard your heart and am waiting here
with someone I have taken to guide you the way

We are ready to receive you,
just look this way
as you go weary from pain
may your spirit swell far above
to join the man you love.

———————————

Married since 1984 to my husband, Tom and we have two
children, Andrew and Allison that amaze us everyday.
Allpoetry.com/Mommy_Bear

[Adelina Morris]

True Peace

Having peace,
isn't when someone
loves you.
Having peace is when
you love yourself.

My name is Adelina Morris. I am from California. I enjoy writing and I love that people can relate to what I write. I try to inspire and give to the paper 100% of my heart. Allpoetry.com/nicoleray91

[Linda Burns]

Ah, the Poet (Just Your Love)

Ah, the Poet is a lover
but he's shy to a degree
so he puts his love in verse
and holds it out to you and me.

And he pretends it doesn't matter
if you like it or you don't
But it does.
It is your love that he wants.

Just your love
Not the money or the fame
Just your love
You don't have to know his name
Just your love
That is all he needs
Just your love

The Poet sits in drafty chamber
He wants to be alone
And he is
Except for his Muse there on his shoulder.

Sometimes she holds him by his heart
Sometimes she holds him by his crotch
you can tell which one

if you care to watch.

The poet bleeds on scraps of paper
and his blood there become word
Then he passes it on to you
hoping your heart will be stirred.

For he feels that he is nothing
if he can't make you see
that a poet is what he
was born to be

And he wants your love
not the money or the fame
Just your love
You don't have to know his name
Just your love
That is all he needs
Just your love

The poet cries on table napkins
and his tears turn into rhyme
He loves this.
It's how he wants to spend his time.

'cause he's a poet, he can't help it
and if he is to live
we must let him offer
all he has to give.

The poet washes his soul and his spirit
and indeed maintains his years
with the words on the paper
and the thanks he thinks he hears

So lets try to give him a little credit
when a little credit is owed
and watch him bloom
at the tribute we bestowed

Behold the Lover Poet
See the smile upon his lips
When we love him, he lights up
In a way we cant eclipse

Let us touch him only gently
for while his body may not break
his spirit might and that's
a chance I will not take.

He wants your love
not the money or the fame
Just your love
You don't have to know his name
Just your love
That is all he needs
Just your love

I have been writing poetry for 59 of my 71 years. My muse is not faithful and abandons me at times but so far, she has always come back. Allpoetry.com has been an invaluable outlet. Allpoetry.com/lindaburns

[Luke Smith]

Snow-globe Eyes

What are you thankful for?
Im thankful for the tired eyes and misjudged time
That place we thought we'd reach in our lives

Breathe...
Deep inner tones soothe your bones
Think of brilliant swirls of blue
Caressing the world anew
Who would have ever knew
There'd be someone as beautiful as you

Dive...
Right into my water of healing
The soft array of waves are appealing
Your eyes soften the darkest of nights
Like a flame i need to you to see without light
A brain like yours with insatiable insight

I miss the summer breeze and sunburnt knees
In the blazing heat, we relax our feet
So take a seat
Sit back, unwind
As here i resign
With you at my side
Then I stare into your snowglobe eyes
And inside the world goes by

Everything ceases with the time
Of snowflake pieces left to lie
Stars fall when i see you cry
Catch everyone because theyre mine
And every time i try
I can't be with you my world has died

_____

Luke is a 20 year old from Merseyside, England
He enjoys skateboarding, writing and living a free life.
420 Allpoetry.com/Schmiddo

[Lisa F. Raines]

Unprecedented President

A President
without precedent
leaves us reticent,
hesitant, and with
a trillion dollar deficit.

My people, my people,
What have you done!
Conjured the devil
in each lie he spun.

More than nine a day
And increasing now,
With more than
nineteen by the
end of this reign.

We know he's not
heaven sent,
more Maleficent
than Magnificent.

With all of his adjectives,
his superlatives, and
exaggerations, he hides
his obfuscations,

and turns the mirror on us,

What has happened to our
society that we can be so easily
lead by such mendacity --
What is it in that looking glass
that so many see?

AlisRamie is from North Carolina, USA.
Interests include: philosophy, history, international relations,
poetry, art, design, jazz, funk, and some good old soul.
Allpoetry.com/AlisRamie

[Chloe Liggett]

More faith than Knowledge based

The mind can be both
an Inescapable curse,
but also an unstoppable force.
Whenever you tell yourself you can,
It becomes an issue.

You still need to make a plan.
When something is important,
It will find its time and place.

You have to understand to succeed
it must be more of faith,
than knowledge based.
We are not always going to have all the answers.

So let the mind play,
as I daze off and see Arcades
and games to play.
Have great faith when you pray.
You'll feel a lot more accomplished.
and get a lot more done that way.

Chloe Liggett is from Chillicothe, Oh. She enjoys writing
poetry, meditation, and art. To calm down, she often takes
bubble baths or counsels others through their problems.
Allpoetry.com/Chloe_Liggett

[Laura Lane]

Grandma

She is a sign of
strength
wisdom
hope
and peace.

She has fought her own wars
and conquered, more than she will ever tell.
She keeps all of that hidden
And to herself.

She will only show you the good
But never the bad.
She will wipe away your tears
Whenever you are sad.

She is the root
of the tree
the reason you are here.

For my grandma was a inspiration to us and we will forever
hold her dear.

To mom- mom whom we lost. She battled so much, and was so strong and caring. She is my inspiration to this poem. My maiden name is Laura Hall..I am from a small town Defiance pa..I have been writing poems, since i was a teenager..My poetry helps me express myself and i enjoy doing it. I also love to paint.
Allpoetry.com/Laura_Lee_Lane

[Joanne Formica]

The World Within

I've been lost in the world, my whole life.
The voices within leave me pondering...
Who I am
Who I am,
Who am I?
I'm being judged by the world in my head
and the world outside.
Someone save me from myself
I'm dangerous to me.
Am I accepted-do I fit in?
I have to learn what I got
and who I am.
The world outside can be harsh and cruel,
But the world inside is even more cruel and harsh.
It's unaccepting and unavailable.
The world outside judges by what it sees,
The world within judges by what it feels...
Feelings of disgust, disappointment and despair
run rampant.
The world outside can be forgiving,
The world within is relentless and unforgiving.
I can escape the world outside,
But the world within holds me captive
A prisoner in my own mind....
And leaves me pondering
Who I am

Who I am
Who am I?

Jo Mama is from Ohio, A grateful Grandma of four little angels. I write poetry to express my feelings, my desires, my pain and my hopes. Allpoetry.com/Jo_mama

[Julie Radford]

Hands of Fate

On a lonely hill, lies a lonely house.
Trapped in a mind, brilliant, but tearing itself apart.
Denied that, which it was gifted.
A goddess, locked in a dungeon, cell doors are wide open.
No one can reach her. No one can reach…her.

In a time long ago.
When a lonely woman, was a joy to know.
She painted the world with magic, only those gifted would
understand it.

The lonely hill? A magnificent thing.
Energy, and life, but that was then.
Twisted is the fate of neglect, and love, and the essence of
life, slips through.

The lonely house is the saddest thing.
Inside the walls, are paintings that she did.
Frozen in time, when it was worth her time.
She walks, a shadow, and hidden.

Trapped is her gift.
In a mind, that just won't quit.
I cannot paint.
My hands…. They shake.

I live with two boys, and two dogs, Tizer, and Pepsi, why the name Tizermax. I live in the UK, near Sherwood Forest, and the legends of Robin Hood. My mind races with stories, and poems. Allpoetry.com/Tizermax

[Owen Nicholls]

Mr Anderson

And here's to you, Mr. Anderson
The Oracle loves you more than you will know (Wo, wo,
wo)
God bless you please, Mr. Anderson
Thc Matrix holds a place for those who pray
(Hey, hey, hey...its where you'll stay)

We'd like to know a little bit about you for our files
We'd like to help you learn to help yourself
Look around you, all you see are sympathetic eyes
Stroll around the grounds until you feel at home.

And here's to you, Mr. Anderson
The Oracle loves you more than you will know (Wo, wo,
wo)
God bless you please, Mr. Anderson
The Matrix holds a place for those who pray
(Hey, hey, hey...its where you'll stay)

Hide it in a hiding place where no one ever goes
Put it in your pantry with your cupcakes
It's a little secret, just the Andersons' affair
Most of all, you've got to hide it from Morpheus

Coo, coo, ca-choo, Mr Anderson
The Oracle loves you more than you will know (Wo, wo,

wo)
God bless you please, Mr. Anderson
The Matrix holds a place for those who pray
(Hey, hey, hey...its where you'll stay)

Sitting on a sofa on a Sunday afternoon
Going to the zion debate
Laugh about it, shout about it
When you've got to choose
Ev'ry way you look at it, you lose

Where have they gone, Neo and Trinity
Zion turns its lonely eyes to you (Woo, woo, woo)
What's that you say, Mr. Anderson
The One has left and gone away.
(Hey, hey, hey...in the matrix he'll stay)

Apologies to Paul Simon. Sung to the tune of Mrs Robinson
in a Agent Smith drawl. I'm an I.T. support guy finding an
writing outlet from his day to day grind. Poetry is my outlet
for up celebration and rages of life.
Allpoetry.com/Owen_Nicholls

[Claire O Dwyer]

This Girl

This girl can you see beyond her insecurity?
The darkness the pain she's hurt once again.
Its all gotten so much but she never gave up,she tried to stay
strong but still things went wrong.

Her head is down,her back is sore she has scars aching from
inside her soul.
Her eyes,they could hold her story but she physically has
lost her energy to be happy.

Does anyone really know how to help her and become the
girl she was, a girl who saw her future through her eyes but
now its blocked with fog from devastating times.

She loved,she was happy why did this be?
Why did they take away her destiny?
It wasn't their choice,wasn't their right but they ruined a big
part of her life.
She had dreams,she had hopes all that were broke, why did a
good person be made to feel bad. She couldn't show her face,
she didn't feel the same, they stole her character made her a
shame.

Now as she walks and looks left to right, she believes in the
rumors and what they have done, to the extent of feeling she
might as-well take the bullet and be gone.

Why did this girl who had her life and love, have to experience all the things they had done. It was horrible it destroyed her and their happy they won.
Yet another person's life controlled by the wrong.

Now as you look at her can anyone understand, how it feels having their life destroyed in the wrong hands.
She still lives her life day by day but do you think her past will ever go away?
She still cry's she still hurts but her happiness is coming first, now she can see that she deserves to be happy.

Past will remain but her future withholds.
She won't let what they done from keeping her from moving on...

———————————

Claire O Dwyer from Ireland. A poem about how bullying can affect someone emotionally but also how strength can overcome anything. Allpoetry.com/Claireod

[Jessica Hughes]

Fly with Wings

Black tears fallen behind your eyes.
Absent mindedly reminding you of all heard lies.
Not something that you've expressed that way.
But how could they not see it in your eyes everyday?
Stand up right, and move on.
Pain doesn't die when you're gone.
Just split into pieces and handed off to those who meant the
most of all.
That's not what I wanted for them, or for me to make that
call. Listening to the dark voices that hide in my head,
Make it hard to lay down for bed.
Can't you hear the sound of the past?
Throwing it up, screaming, happiness will NEVER last?
You don't deserve them, or the joy they bring.
You've been too messed up, to ever fly with wings.
Every bad thought, rings true.
Because of this, I'm drifting from you.
I just need you to hold on.
Wait on me until the pain is gone.
Love me for who I am, let me know I'm worth a damn.

Jessica is from Pensacola, Florida. Writing has been a gift
I'm always willing to share. Dedicated to Robby, who never
got his chance to shine. Allpoetry.com/Jaded_Willow

[Ariel Rosewrite]
A Dying Man Called Freddy

My love for you is eternal
I will love you even after
the sun's flames no longer burn and
all the oceans run dry
Even if the heavens roll up like scrolls
and all the stars come crashing down around us
I will still have passion for you
Father of my children
Guardian of my heart
I am nothing without you and
I will cross oceans of time
just to be with you again and
when I see you and you see me
I will know you and you will know me

I'm from San Benito, Texas. Poetry became a passion after
suffering a personal loss. South Padre Island remote quiet
areas are a source for inspiration Allpoetry.com/Rosewrite7

[Anthony Edward Parker]

Finding Equilibrium Through The

Depths Of Solitude

Socially unorganized, I place critics down a size
Standing with preferred confidence gave me insight
Partially adapted from the root of fear
I sometimes hear my inner voice remarking that my time is
near

Position to overcome challenging courses
By altering our contained nature to make stronger choices
Often at the mill I witness the loud of noises
I either adjust or continue breathing in the poison and drown
in my salty ocean

Maybe tears can be manufactured through happy times
Is it weird I fake my laughter through your own surprises

Some may question my ability to think and process
I reveal the sources to my brightened conscience

Assemble the many gears we set in stone
Ever wonder what's it's like to be thrown?

My past creates a memory lane for me to see
I rather improve my empathy willing to still believe

In love with a spirit because I glance swiftly while there is
no in sight
Passport to find true family as I hunch over my seat, in
hopes to discover actual happiness during a safe flight

I settled among 10 siblings without parental guidance.
Practically raising me military minded, I found methods that
helped cure depressive symptoms. Through writing it allows
to me display who I am. Allpoetry.com/Edward_P.

[Anthony Edward Parker]
A Hurricane On The Coast

Vision is watery, eyes completely flushed
Viewing the solid ground, shoe kicking the dust
Limiting correspondence with those who I struggle to trust
Head Hotter than the Earth's crust, I bond with the flames for
fun
Rejection is rough, especially when your reflection stares at
you because you're the only one

Fiddle with this pen as if I'm going to be famous someday
Extend each vocal to fully grasp what consist of my pain
Some angel's say I'll breeze through the thunder and rain
This is what I gain from rearranging my life around, to be
vomiting a crucial weight
If I express the motive for freshness, God might notice my
patience
While I'm waiting for a key to see the other side of the gate
My entire soul I give, but sick of my current suffering,
feeding off the negative trait

Obtaining a family ticket to a new world
Probably the only place I'll ever meet a girl
Sometimes my mental state is on the north pole
But soon I'll propose to a heavenly ghost
A spot for Edward to go forward
Metaphorically a cell that consistently grows

I settled among 10 siblings without parental guidance. Practically raising me military minded, I found methods that helped cure depressive symptoms. Through writing it allows to me display who I am. Allpoetry.com/Edward_P.

[Lisa F. Raines]

Memorial of Mary

Please envelop me
   in your grief, and
help me maintain
   my true belief.

Provide our souls
   some sweet relief;
we know too well
   our life is brief.

We cry and try
   to bury and lie,
deny, defy and decry,
   our states--our fates--
but in the end,
   all must leave this life.

It's those who grieve,
   here behind,
we hope to receive
   in God's own time.

Providing our souls
   such sweet relief,
coming to God
   with full belief.

AlisRamie is from North Carolina, USA.

Interests include: philosophy, history, international relations, poetry, art, design, jazz, funk, and some good old soul.

Allpoetry.com/AlisRamie

[Lisa F. Raines]

The Tick Talk of the Clock

The tick talk of the
incessant clock

remInds us, designs us,
defincs and
confines us.

It binds us to the
artificial construct,
and, blinds us to
our own slow walk

toward time, and
what we forgot.

The lines of hate
they had wrought

divides us, hides us,
abides and derides us...

No truth was ever found
in having lied to us...

Testing our faith,

in all our haste,
we find our fate
in the great debate.

AlisRamie is from North Carolina, USA.
Interests include: philosophy, history, international relations, poetry, art, design, jazz, funk, and some good old soul.
Allpoetry.com/AlisRamie

[Robert M.]

Cocaine lust

That first anticipation of what's about to be. Slight nervous
reaction. Jittery.
Consociate hunger, with an apprehensive edge, yet
fullfillment is deep as ritually prepared is the pledge.
Antecedent excitement soon dominates thought. Preparation
complete, pleasure now sought.

That first sharp intake...that first sharp intake. Breath stolen.
World awakes. Unabashed pleasure, as the wave overtakes.
Mandatory smile, neurons quake. Laughter now deep. No
more thoughts of sleep.

Consumption resumption, supercharged function. Algorithm
Repeated. Sensibility defeated.
Sharpest of inhales, shudder of curtness,
Inner voice yearns more, cannot close that door. That sharp
spark of neurons and smile of the victim, fully enslaved to
this Modern contagion. Cyclopean hunger, defeats all
thoughts of slumber.

Conversation repeated, intellect defeated.
Time without form as transition towards dawn. Inexorable
conclusion of a night with no form.

finallly gone, yet always want more.
That Loveliest of birdsong, a fearful throng.

Realisation of the hour, night turned sour.
So tired in my head but never to bed.
Close eyes so Tired but my world is wired.
Fearful for sleep but never go deep.

Rich healing slumber, tonight I am poor.
Broken promise to make, never,ever, no more!

———————————

Robert is from the UK. I am rediscovering a love of words that I had many years ago as a schoolchild. I am getting much more experience from life nowadays.
Allpoetry.com/Lascielstry